LIFE IN THE SPIRIT

THEOLOGICAL MEDITATIONS, edited by Hans Küng

Previously Published:

Freedom Today by Hans Küng

The Unknown God by Joseph Möller,
Herbert Haag and Gotthold Hasenhüttl

Belief Today by Karl Rahner, S.J.

THEOLOGICAL MEDITATIONS ·

Life in the Spirit

edited with a Preface by HANS KÜNG

SHEED AND WARD · NEW YORK

Part I was originally published in German
under the title Ihr alle seid Geistliche,
© Benziger Verlag, Einsiedeln, 1964.
It was originally published in English
under the title A Priestly People.
Translated by M. H. Heelan
© Sheed and Ward, Ltd., 1965

Part II was originally published in German
under the title Wander Christlicher Spiritualität,
© Benziger Verlag, Einsiedeln, 1967.
Translated by Fred Wieck
© Sheed and Ward, Inc., 1968

Part III was originally published in German
under the title Der Zölibat,
© Benziger Verlag, Einsiedeln, 1965.
Translated by Carole Tansley
© Sheed and Ward, Ltd., 1967

231.3

Library of Congress Catalog Card Number 68–14539

Nihil Obstat:
    Thomas J. Beary
    Censor Librorum
Imprimatur:
    ✠ Robert F. Joyce
    Bishop of Burlington
    November 28, 1967

Manufactured in the United States of America

Preface

Who in the Church is in possession of the *Spirit?* Since the high Middle Ages, the "Holy Spirit" has in many quarters been thought to reside virtually in the hierarchy, the clergy. There has been a tendency to neglect the universal spiritual dimension of the whole Church, of the entire people of God. Only the monks were leading a truly "spiritual life," and only clerics had "spirituality." They alone were truly in possession of the Spirit, they alone were spiritual men—*spirituales*, in the Latin. The word "spiritual" came to mean the same thing as the word "religious," and to be applied to the priestly orders.

How complete a misunderstanding this is of the Pauline antithesis of "Spirit" and "flesh"—a misunderstanding fostered mainly by the rejection of matter and body in Plato and neo-Platonism. In contrast with the clergy, the laity were considered "men of the flesh"—the *left* side of Christ's body, as they were also called in the Middle Ages. For they were in the bondage of marriage and worldly possessions, while separation from the body, from marriage, and from woman—that is, celibacy—had become the mark of the "spiritual life," the "life in the Spirit and according to the Spirit." Only in the last few decades has it become necessary to develop, albeit painfully, something like a "lay spirituality" (which is in part still rather puny).

But today we in the Church are newly aware that according to the New Testament *all* faithful baptized Christians are filled with the Spirit. All Christians, and not just a particular group of ecstatics, "spiritual" men or ascetics, not just a particular group of sacred office-holders—no, all men who have faith are men of the Spirit and ministers, and are called to the ministry. *Every* Christian is a man of the Spirit insofar as he has died to the flesh and to sin, and has received God's Spirit. *Every* Christian *is called* to be a minister, a man of the Spirit, insofar as he overcomes sin in his life, lives in the Spirit, and bears spiritual fruit. The "flesh," according to Paul himself, means generally the man who is far away from God and is opposed to God, the man who lets himself be moved and dominated not by God's Spirit but by his own drives, appetites, and urges. The "works of the flesh," according to Paul, are not just fornication and debauchery, but the sins of the spirit as well. All this is the subject of the First Meditation.

A second consideration follows: a *change in Christian spirituality* has in fact taken place! We can no longer think of Christian spiritual life exclusively in terms of spiritual, religious exercises. Prayer will still be important in our day, of course, more important even than in the past, when it had become largely mechanical. But the "life according to the Spirit," to Jesus' Spirit, today finds its expression most of all in the living love of our brother. The "spiritual life" may not take place inside a religious preserve set apart and protected by a sacral shell—it must be lived in the midst of the world.

Worldly piety means that our daily life must become service to God, the world itself become the place of our encounter with God. I must find God in the world, here where I stand, and such as I am, as the man I am to be fully, to become fully. This is the theme of the Second Meditation.

By the same token, we have also gained a new awareness of the problems of celibacy. Let no high-toned theological speculation becloud the fact that total surrender to God is just as possible for married people—each according to his vocation, his own charisma. The gospels know of a personal vocation to celibacy in the service of mankind: Jesus and Paul are its great exemplars even for our day. And such a vocation is and always will be a great and wonderful thing. But both Jesus and Paul explicitly give to every man his full freedom: "He who is able to receive this, let him receive it" (Mt. 19:12); "each has his own special gift from God, one of one kind and one of another" (1 Cor. 7:7). This explicitly granted freedom, this celibacy by virtue of a free charisma, is denied—as we have again come to realize—by a general law of celibacy, compelling every member of the clergy to receive what he is perhaps not able to receive. Indeed, Peter and the apostles were married and remained so, as perfect followers of Jesus—and for centuries they set the example for the spiritual leaders of the Christian communities. But celibacy, originally a freely chosen state which had its place especially in monastic communities, became in later centuries transformed into the explicit prohibition to marry, and was extended to all clerics and in part forced upon them. The story of how the law of celibacy was introduced is not a pretty story—as the Third Meditation makes clear. In our own day, however, since the Council, the opinion is gaining ground within the Catholic

Church, among priests and laity, that this radical legal inter-
ference with the personal rights of man is a violation not only
of the gospel and of the original and free structure of the
Church, but also of our present concept of individual freedom. The Church must now pay dearly for the fact that in
past centuries the "spiritual life" was given such a narrow
meaning.

The facts are known; we shall just list them briefly: *first*,
the Church is losing candidates for the priesthood—often of
very high qualifications—in numbers which in recent years
have reached a frightening level, candidates whom she needs
today more than ever. *Second*, the numbers of those who
leave the priestly office after ordination, or get involved in
hopeless difficulties, now run in the tens of thousands. (There
are now before the Curia four thousand requests from priests
for permission to marry; it is estimated in Rome that about
10% of the entire priesthood are suspended because of failure
to keep the obligation of celibacy, 4,000 of them in France,
15,000—out of a total of 70,000—in Italy, and from 30,000
to 40,000 throughout the world.) And *third*, despite the often
extreme shortage of priests, and the universally evident fact
that the clergy is over-age, the question of married or unmarried clergy has taken precedence over the Church's pri-
mary obligation to provide the communities with pastors.
Other points could be argued. In any case, the Catholic
Church will not know peace until celibacy is once again left
to the free decision of the individual, and the canon on
celibacy, which was introduced under the most dubious circumstances, is revoked. The Third Meditation, which takes
an historical approach, is an urgent invitation to do so.

Is the post-Conciliar Church retrenching? True, there are

a number of time-bound, needless, even detrimental aspects
which are indeed being reduced—not only in the interest of
modernization, but because the original Christian message
demands it. But in making this effort, to translate the original
Christian message into the terms of today, we are not retrenching but on the contrary forging ahead: our demands
today are not less but greater—we demand a more radical
commitment to God, and thus to man.

HANS KÜNG

Contents

THE ONE PRIESTHOOD

by *Karl Hermann Schelkle*

TRANSLATED BY M. H. HEELAN

Introduction

Constantine's decision, for political as well as religious reasons, to make Christianity the predominant religion of the Roman Empire led to measures aimed at discouraging the various pagan cults. Reluctance to renounce the public worship of the ancient gods became liable to legal penalties. In these circumstances it paid to be a Christian. Soon a flood of pagans streamed into the Church of confessors and martyrs. It was only natural that very many of these recruits to the Faith lacked the earnestness and fervor of the existing Christian communities. Some of the older Christians, therefore, fearing they might be hindered in professing and practising their religion in the former, stricter way to which they were accustomed, separated from the "half-Christian" newcomers. They gave out that they were "Christians of the spirit" who proposed to live according to the Holy Spirit and not according to the "flesh" and the "world," as, to their mind, the others were doing. "Flesh" and "world" here should, of course, be taken in the biblical sense as simply meaning human, earthly desires and aspirations. All the same, the title adopted by these groups of older Christians implied the high, exclusive claim that they were the true heirs of the Christian spiritual heritage. They favored the monastic life and often left the amenity of wealthy cities to go and live in barren deserts. Many entered the ranks of the priesthood. One of the results of all this was that the use of "spiritual" as a personal qualification eventually came to be applied exclusively to priests and monks.

The young Church, stepping fresh and confident out of the pages of the New Testament, had a different view: *all* Christians are endowed, nay *filled*, with the Holy Spirit, and because of this general gift of the Spirit *all* Christians can be called spiritual. St. Paul says: "And we impart this in words . . . taught by the Spirit, interpreting spiritual truths to those who possess the Spirit" (1 Cor. 2:13),[1] and again, ". . . if a man is overtaken in any trespass, you who are spiritual should restore him in a spirit of gentleness" (Gal. 6:1).

Teaching and preaching in the New Testament on the subject of the Holy Spirit are incomparably richer than those current among us today. In the Apostles' Creed we say, "I believe in the Holy Ghost [or Holy Spirit]." In the Gloria we declare our faith in the Holy Spirit as a person of the Blessed Trinity, thus: "Glory be to the Father and to the Son and to the Holy Ghost." But when we think of the Holy Spirit do we have in mind only a divine person infinitely far away? The New Testament, however, has many allusions to the proximity and the presence of the Holy Spirit and the fruit we derive therefrom. To the presence of the Holy Spirit the Church owes her spiritual wealth and privileges, her supernatural strength and divine character. And what is the inmost being and life of every member of the redeemed People of God but the Holy Spirit dwelling within us?

The Spirit is promised to all

The Acts of the Apostles describe the outpouring of the Holy
Spirit at Pentecost which ushered in the Christian Church
(2: 1–47). The biblical account of this profuse manifestation
of the Spirit teems with striking words and ideas. Indeed, one
cannot help wondering how the sacred writer found words to
express such profound ideas so vividly and so exactly. We
know from research into the history of biblical language that
even the idea of spirit, let alone the words to express its manifestations, had a relatively small place in the Hellenistic en-
vironment of the New Testament. Israel, on the other hand,
speaks of the Spirit of God on the very first page of holy writ:
"In the beginning . . . darkness was upon the face of the deep;
and the Spirit of God [meaning, presumably, a mighty, creative wind] was moving over the face of the waters" (Gen.
1:2). From the very outset the Spirit of God is seen in the divine creative action in nature. "Thou didst send forth thy
Spirit, and it formed them" (Jdt. 16:14). "The Spirit of the
Lord has filled the world" (Wisd. of Sol. 1:7). God's breath
and spirit are man's very life. According to the account of crea-

tion, "the Lord God formed man of dust from the ground, and breathed into his nostrils the breath of life" (Gen. 2:7). Every man can say: "The spirit of God has made me, and the breath of the Almighty gives me life" (Job 28:4). The human spirit is a perpetually renewed gift from God to man, whereby man's life is sustained; it is, so to speak, a participation in the Spirit of God.

The Spirit of the Lord is active all through the history of Israel. In the earlier period the prodigious deeds of Israel's remarkable heroes were ascribed to the presence of the Spirit within them. The Spirit of God rested on Moses who was God's friend and Israel's lawgiver and ruler (Num. 11:25). For centuries Israel was at war with the Philistines. The Spirit of God raised up leaders and champions from the Chosen People and made them mighty warriors; under their leadership Israel fought until the threat from a stronger enemy was removed. Again and again the historical books of the Bible which deal with this period tell how the Spirit of the Lord came upon Israel's heroes and kings. This was the case with Joshua (Num. 27:18), Gideon (Judg. 6:34), Jephthah (Judg. 11:29), Samson (Judg. 14:6, 19), Saul (1 Sam. 11:6) and David (1 Sam. 16:13).

It was the Spirit, too, who appointed those who were to be Israel's teachers. The Bible says that the great prophets Elijah and Elisha were endowed with the Spirit (2 Kgs. 2:15). The prophet Micah says of himself: "But as for me, I am filled with power, with the Spirit of the Lord" (Mic. 3:8). The saddest and darkest days in Israel's history were those that saw Jerusalem laid in ruins by her enemies and her people carried off into captivity and exile in Babylon (585–538 B.C.). But God raised up among the enslaved captives the mysterious

"Servant of God" of the second part of the Book of Isaiah to exhort and console them; of him God himself says: "I have put my Spirit upon him, he will bring forth justice to the nations" (Isa. 42:1). And the Servant of God says of himself:

> The Spirit of the Lord God is upon me,
> because the Lord has anointed me
> to bring good tidings to the afflicted;
> he has sent me to bind up the broken-
> hearted, to proclaim liberty to the
> captives, and the opening of the prison to
> those who are bound. [Isa. 61:1f.]

The Spirit also teaches wisdom and the Spirit of wisdom is a kindly spirit (Wisd. of Sol. 1:6). Ultimately Israel realizes that it is the Spirit who inspires and directs the just man. The psalmist cries out: "Take not thy holy Spirit from me . . . and uphold me with a willing spirit" (Ps. 51:11–12), and again, "Let thy good spirit lead me on a level path!" (Ps. 143:10). But the time comes at last when the Old Dispensation looks forward to the universal outpouring of the Spirit which is to mark the final stage of revelation, the time of salvation, the messianic age when the New Dispensation comes into being. Isaiah, looking forward to that time, says:

> Thus says the Lord . .
> I will pour water on the thirsty land
> and streams on the dry ground;
> I will pour my Spirit upon your descendants,
> and my blessing on your offspring. [Isa. 44:3]

Israel firmly believes that the words of her prophets must be fulfilled, and the prophets tell her: "My Spirit abides among you; fear not" (Hag. 2:5), and, "Not by might, nor by power, but by my Spirit, says the Lord of Hosts" (Zech. 4:6).

After the return from Babylon and up to the coming of Christ, the Jews pinned their faith on the promised Messiah. They also clung steadfastly to the belief that with the coming of the Messiah and salvation, the Spirit of God would be showered upon his Chosen People and they would all be made new. The Messiah himself would possess the Spirit in all its fullness, with all its various gifts:

> And the Spirit of the Lord shall rest upon him,
> the spirit of wisdom and understanding,
> the spirit of counsel and might,
> the spirit of knowledge and the fear of the Lord.
> [Isa. 11:2]

By virtue of the Spirit the Israelites would all become prophets:

> ... I will pour out my spirit on all flesh;
> your sons and your daughters shall prophesy,
> ... And it shall come to pass that all who call upon
> the name of the Lord shall be delivered. [Joel
> 2:28, 30]

The diffusion of the Spirit would lead to the moral renewal of the people. The Spirit would make them holy and bring them into high favor with the Lord: "A new heart I will give you, and a new spirit I will put within you . . . and cause you to walk in my statutes and be careful to observe my ordinances

. . . you shall be my people, and I will be your God" (Ezek. 36:26–8). True, in the time immediately preceding the coming of Christ, we find Israel complaining that hopes of the Spirit are fading; that Israel is no longer worthy to receive the Spirit. Religious teachers and devout Jews lamented that the children of Israel no longer had a prophet to guide them and did not know whether they would ever get another; on the death of Haggai, Zechariah and Malachi, the last of the prophets, they feared that the Spirit of God would cease to appear in Israel. The more they read the promises in the sacred books of the Old Testament, the more they yearned for the dawn of the new era when the Spirit would be poured out upon them. Israel was now bowed down again under a foreign yoke, this time the unyielding yoke of Roman rule. The impotence of her people increased their longing for the fulfillment of the great vision of the prophet Ezekiel which he had once related to the exiles in Babylon:

The hand of the Lord was upon me, and he brought me out by the Spirit of the Lord, and set me down in the midst of the plain; it was full of bones. And he led me round among them; and behold, there were very many upon the plain; and lo, they were very dry . . . he said to me, "Prophesy to these bones, and say to them, O dry bones, hear the word of the Lord. Thus says the Lord God to these bones: Behold, I will cause spirit to enter you, and you shall live . . ." So I prophesied as I was commanded; and as I prophesied, there was . . . a rattling; and the bones came together, bone to its bone. And as I looked, there were sinews on them, and flesh had come upon them, and skin had covered them . . . Then he said to me, "Prophesy to the spirit. . . . Come from the four winds,

O spirit, and breathe upon these slain, that they may live." . . .
and the spirit came into them, and they lived, and stood upon
their feet, an exceedingly great host. Then he said to me: ". . .
these bones are the whole house of Israel . . . they say, 'Our
bones are dried up, and our hope is lost; we are clean cut off!'
Therefore . . . say to them, Thus says the Lord God: . . . I will
put my Spirit within you, and you shall live, and I will place
you in your own land . . . I, the Lord, have spoken, and I have
done it . . ." [Ezek. 37:1–14]

In Ezekiel's vision, as in the vision of creation (Gen. 1:2), it
will be observed that the Spirit is typified by a mighty creative
wind.

These prophecies and hopes of salvation are not fully and
finally realized in either the New Testament or the Church
of today. Their perfect fulfillment will only be attained in that
new creation promised for the day of the Lord.

All are endowed with the Spirit

What we have just said must not, however, be allowed to ob-
scure the message of the New Testament and its gospel, which
is this: The hope and expectation of so many generations of
Jewish believers now *begins* to be fulfilled. The Spirit of God
is again manifest and active among God's people. Jesus the
Messiah is conceived by the Spirit (Mt. 1:18). At his baptism
the Spirit descends upon him (Mt. 3:16). By the power of
the Spirit of God he overcomes the malignant evil spirits and
by so doing announces the advent of the kingdom of God:
"But if it is by the Spirit of God that I cast out demons, then
the kingdom of God has come upon you" (Mt. 12:28). The
disciples of the Messiah were also filled with the Spirit. The
Acts of the Apostles (2:1–4) gives the following description
of the first Christian Pentecost:

*When the day of Pentecost had come, they were all together
in one place. And suddenly a sound came from heaven like the
rush of a mighty wind, and it filled all the house where they
were sitting. And there appeared to them tongues as of fire,*

distributed and resting on each one of them. And they were all filled with the Holy Spirit and began to speak in other tongues, as the Spirit gave them utterance.

There were about 120 persons present.

This is a typical illustration of the activity and nature of the Spirit. It is not something which is innate in man, such as a natural faculty; it is a supernatural God-given gift that defies explanation and can only be inadequately described in human language. All the assembled disciples—and not only the apostles (as our artists usually seem to think)—the entire Christian Church, in fact, are witnesses and active participants in the scene at Pentecost, and all of them receive the Spirit. Once again (as in Gen. 1:2; cf. Jn. 3:8) the Spirit appears as a tempestuous wind. The whole house is filled with it, just as the whole world will be filled with the Spirit. The fire is a symbol of the blaze of glory in which God dwells. Like a sheet of flame from on high it descends upon the band of disciples, leaving none untouched. The revelation which the descriptive imagery of this astounding event is intended to convey is that *each* individual receives the gift of the Spirit, while the Spirit nevertheless remains one and undivided. As St. Paul says: "There are diversities of graces, but only one and the same Spirit" (1 Cor. 12:4). The fiery tongues of the Spirit produce the other, new tongues of the disciples. The receptive listeners, hearing the ecstatic speech of the disciples, take this as proof that the Spirit has been poured out upon them and that the good news they bring is true. Out of the Spirit streams the word of God, soon to penetrate to the ends of the earth. All the disciples are appointed to proclaim the good news; it is the duty of every Christian to tell men of Christ. This day of

Pentecost is primarily the fulfillment of Christ's promise to the young Christian community (Acts 1:8) that the Holy Spirit would fit them for their mission; but from now on it will also mark the coming of the New Dispensation which is to fulfill the promises made to the Hebrews under the Old Covenant. The first apostolic sermon handed down to us in the New Testament is that delivered by Peter on the day of Pentecost. In it he quotes the prophecy of Joel (2:28–32) that (in the "last days") the Lord will pour out his Spirit on all flesh. Peter assures the polyglot crowd of Jewish listeners that Joel's prophecy is now fulfilled (Acts 2:17–21).

In both the Old and New Testaments the same dual conception of the working of the Holy Spirit is apparent. In the Old Testament it is primarily the power to perform things beyond man's ordinary capacity, but sometimes it means strength of faith in God. The New Testament mostly thinks of it as a miraculous power, but occasionally—and particularly in St. Paul's letters—it is spoken of as the power manifest every day in the life of the Christian, enabling him to live in faith and in the love of God.

One book—the Acts of the Apostles—makes a special point of recounting the marvellous gifts and acts of the Holy Spirit. It first tells of the wonderful outpouring of the Spirit at Pentecost (Acts 2:1–13). A new sign—a trembling of the earth—heralds a subsequent coming of the Spirit upon the Christian community (Acts 4:31); it would seem as if the earth were unable to bear the weight of the heavenly powers. There are many other signs and wonders (Acts 2:43; 5:15). The imparting of the Spirit continued to bring the gift of tongues (Acts 10:46; 19:6). The Acts of the Apostles and Paul's letters frequently mention this gift of tongues; the persons who re-

ceive it are thrown into a state of ecstasy and utter sounds
and words unintelligible to listeners and themselves; the
tongue appears, in such cases, to speak of itself and to be beyond the control of its owner. To understand and explain
what such speech signified, a special gift of interpretation was
granted to some by the Holy Spirit. Jesus had already promised
that the words with which the Christian missionaries were to
testify when they were brought before their persecutors would
be put into their mouths by the Holy Spirit (Acts 1:8; Mk.
13:11). Stephen the protomartyr became ecstatic under the
influence of the Holy Spirit; he saw the heavens opened and
Christ standing at the right hand of God (Acts 7:55). The
Spirit of the Lord miraculously guided Philip on his mission
(Acts 8:29–39). The prophet Agabus, prompted by the Spirit,
foretold that there would be a great famine (Acts 11:28) and
that Paul would be delivered into the hands of the Gentiles
when he reached Jerusalem (Acts 21:11). Paul himself, by
the power of the Spirit, inflicted a supernatural penalty on
the magician who opposed the preaching of the gospel (Acts
13:9). As they went from city to city the apostles received in-
struction and guidance from the Holy Spirit (Acts 10:19;
11:12; 16:6f.; 20:22f.; 21:4). Filled with the Holy Spirit, they
bore witness openly and fearlessly, wherever they went, and
their opponents could not withstand the word of the Spirit
(Acts 4:8, 31; 5:3–9; 6:10; 18:25; 19:6).

But there is abundant awareness, too, in the Acts of the
Apostles, that the Spirit is a gift given to the members of the
Church, one and all, and that it is continually active in the
ordinary circumstances of everyday Christian life. The Church
which emerged from Israel grew and "in the comfort of the
Holy Spirit . . . was multiplied"; even the converts from

paganism received the gift of the Spirit (Acts 9:31; 10:45-7).
All are endowed with the Spirit at baptism (Acts 2:38) and
when the hands of the apostles are laid upon them (Acts
8:17). Indeed God gives the Spirit to all who obey him (Acts
5:32). All, therefore, who hear the Church are filled with the
Spirit. And this Spirit is active everywhere, increasing faith
and renewing life. The Holy Spirit's descent upon the disciples
in the form of tongues of fire which rested on all those who
were present must surely indicate that the task of proclaiming
the gospel and the mighty works of the Lord is a task for
every member of the Church (Acts 2:3, 11). The Holy Spirit
raises up prophets and missionaries to bear the divine message
to the end of the earth (Acts 1:8), and he gives them the
courage to "speak the word of God with boldness" (Acts
4:31). In the Acts also he is freely referred to as the Spirit of
wisdom (6:3,10), the Spirit of faith (6:5; 11:24) and the
Spirit of joy (13:52).

That the Spirit is a gift for all is also evident from the
manner in which the Spirit is received. Up to the end of time
it will be possible for the Church to receive the Spirit as truly
as it was received in the remarkable circumstances of the first
Christian Pentecost. God has the sovereign right of direct
communication with man. To any man God can assign any
mission and grant a renewal or increase of the Spirit for the
fulfillment of that mission. But God may also act through the
medium of visible signs or symbols which have conventional
significance. If we were to ask Christians of our time how the
Spirit is received, we should certainly be told that we receive
the Spirit through the sacraments—through baptism in the
first place and later on, by way of renewal and completion,
through the imposition of hands at confirmation (Acts 2:38;

8:17). This is, of course, a correct answer. But the Church also says that a sacrament is efficacious only if rightly received. According to the Acts of the Apostles (2:38; 19:2f.) the Christian community receives the Holy Spirit through baptism and faith. Christ our Lord says the same thing: "He who believes and is baptized will be saved" (Mk. 16:16). Paul says: "For by one Spirit we were all baptized into one body . . . and all were made to drink of one Spirit" (1 Cor. 12:13): and in his Letter to the Galatians (3:14) we are given to understand that we receive the promised Spirit through faith. Sacrament and faith together bring the Spirit to us. In this way the New Testament distinguishes the sacraments from "magic." Magic is an effort to force one's will upon nature, to get material results. With a sacrament the case is different. It has *spiritual* effects and these only if men harmonize their will with God's.

Charisms of the Spirit in everyday life

Let us go through St. Paul's teaching on the subject of the Holy Spirit. Besides developing the theme that the Church is filled with the Holy Spirit, he repeatedly lists the wonderful charisms or gifts which the Spirit bestows on the Church. For example, he says:

To one is given through the Spirit the utterance of wisdom, and to another the utterance of knowledge according to the same Spirit, to another faith by the same Spirit, to another gifts of healing by the one Spirit, to another the working of miracles, to another prophecy, to another the ability to distinguish between spirits, to another various kinds of tongues, to another the interpretation of tongues. All these are inspired by one and the same Spirit, who apportions to each one individually as he wills. [1 Cor. 12:8–11]

Here we find Paul listing not only wonders such as healing-power, the gift of tongues, and prophecy, but charisms that go to the making of the everyday life of a Christian, such as wisdom, knowledge and faith. At the end of the chapter just quoted, Paul exhorts the Corinthians to desire the higher gifts, very earnestly (1 Cor. 12:31). In the two succeeding chapters he deals with two of these higher gifts of the Spirit which every Christian should strive for—love, and the power to interpret the word of God in order to instruct others (1 Cor. 13; 14). Of love he says: "If I speak in the tongues of men and of angels, but have not love, I am a noisy gong or a clanging cymbal" (1 Cor. 13:1). And more valuable than the gift of ecstatic, but incomprehensible, speech is the power to speak to men for their upbuilding and encouragement and consolation (1 Cor. 14:3). On another occasion Paul says that the fruit of the Spirit is "love, joy, peace, patience, kindness, goodness, faithfulness, gentleness, self-control" (Gal. 5:22).

Later on Paul describes and expounds the charisms one by one. The Spirit is the power of faith. To his own faith Paul applies the words of the inspired author of the 116th Psalm; the Apostle writes: "Since we have the same spirit of faith as he had, who wrote, 'I believed, and so I spoke,' we too believe, and so we speak" (2 Cor. 4:13; Ps. 116:10). No man can believe by simply making up his mind he will believe. Faith is infused by the Spirit; it is his gift. The little Christian community at Thessalonica was from the very start beset by many enemies. Paul announced the word of God to them "in power and in the Holy Spirit and with full conviction," and they received the word "in much affliction, [but] with joy inspired by the Holy Spirit" (1 Thess. 1:5f.). It is the Spirit, too, who confers the power to profess, and bear witness to, faith in the word of God, and the power to give ear to the word, take it in, and hold on to it. Only in the Holy Spirit can one profess faith in Jesus as Saviour and Lord and belong to the community of Christ's disciples, for "no one can say 'Jesus is Lord' except by the Holy Spirit" (1 Cor. 12:3). It is through the Spirit that Christian believers become God's children: "You have received the spirit of sonship. When we cry 'Abba! Father!' it is the Spirit himself bearing witness with our spirit that we are children of God . . ." (Rom. 8:15–16; cf. Gal. 4:6). Man can pray only because the Spirit gives him power to do so. Left to himself man would not know how to pray, as he ought, to the God of infinite sanctity, power and love. If it were only a human appeal, it would never be anything but a futile cry into the void. Not so the prayer of the Christian: his prayer is a mysterious communion between God and man wherein God helps out man's insufficiency. The Spirit of God takes hold of our prayer, brings it up to God's throne, and pleads our cause before the Almighty. The Spirit purges it of its imperfections and turns it into a fitting act of adoration and petition. He translates human language into heavenly language. The divine Spirit whom God has given us "intercedes for us with sighs too deep for words" (Rom. 8:26f.). God himself, by means of his Spirit, helps his creatures to bear their burdens.

The Spirit, therefore, lays open man's heart before God, and to God. He also opens man's heart to man's neighbor. Paul depicts the plenitude of the Spirit with which the Church is endowed (1 Cor. 12:4–31). The Spirit, one and undivided, produces many wonderful charisms in the Church. Paul, in his list of them, singles out for special mention those which he describes as "for the common good." To these belong "the utterance of wisdom" and "the utterance of knowledge," that is to say, preaching that proceeds from a deep

insight into the divine mysteries; the "gifts of healing," efficacious for both body and soul; the ability to help the community
in administration or other activities; "prophecy," meaning
utterance in the power of God; and the ability "to distinguish
between spirits," which apparently means a particular aptitude
for pastoral work. In Corinth there were many manifestations
of "speaking in various kinds of tongues." The Corinthians
were greatly impressed by ecstatic speech and gave it a high
place among manifestations of the Spirit. Paul, in his first
Letter to them, thanks God that he "spoke in tongues" more
than any of them, but goes on to say that he would rather
speak five words with his mind, in order to instruct others,
than ten thousand words "in a tongue." He wants them,
therefore, to keep their ecstatic speech within bounds; more
valuable and important than ecstatic speech is the gift of
prophecy—inspired preaching—for prophetic speech is edify-
ing, upbuilding, encouraging and consoling for the Church.
And, he adds, they must strive to excel in building up the
Church (1 Cor. 14:3f., 22–5).

In his Letter to the Romans (12:6–8) Paul again lists the
gifts of the Spirit which the Church possesses. First on his
list is prophecy, the gift of preaching instructive, stimulating,
comforting and healing discourses, full of the inspiration and
power of the Holy Spirit. Then there is teaching, whose major
function in the Church was to explain holy writ and transmit
the apostolic tradition. Paul then mentions concern for one's
inner vocation and external task; giving and sharing-out, acts
of mercy and love, personal and public works of charity; and
zeal and devotion in directing and carrying on the necessary
business of the community. All these various kinds of service
and behavior are summed up in one service, obligatory for

everyone, though the ways in which it may be performed are very diverse—and that is the service of love.

In his Letter to the Galatians, Paul once more describes the new life in the Spirit. Man in his natural state lives under the law of the flesh. "Now the works of the flesh are plain: immorality, impurity, licentiousness, idolatry, sorcery, enmity, strife, jealousy, anger, selfishness, dissension, party spirit, envy, drunkenness, carousing and the like" (Gal. 5:19–21). The works of the flesh would obviously bring ruin upon the community. But when we receive the Spirit we are regenerated and it becomes possible for us to live according to the Spirit. "The fruit of the spirit is love, joy, peace, patience, kindness, goodness, faithfulness, gentleness, self-control" (Gal. 5:22–3). The way of life that is grounded on the Spirit makes for, and means, community among men. When Paul speaks of the *works* of the flesh but of the *fruit* of the Spirit, it may well mean that he used the plural for the former and the singular for the latter in order to stress that the former are man's own works for which he will be held accountable, and the latter is God's gift, which is always the gift of one and the same Spirit, who produces many and diverse effects in those who possess him.

Although all Christians who believe and are baptized receive the Spirit, Paul feels bound to warn the Christians in Corinth that, while they have all received the gift of the Spirit, he must nevertheless address them as "men of the flesh, as babes in Christ" (1 Cor. 3:1), and that because the spiritual side of their nature is not yet sufficiently developed and because theirs is only human wisdom, they do not understand and do not accept the things of God (1 Cor. 13f.). The Christian must "earnestly desire the spiritual gifts" (1 Cor. 14:1).

The gifts are also virtues and the Christian must strive to acquire them. Paul exhorts the Galatians to walk by the Spirit and not to gratify the desires of the flesh (5:16), and later says in the same Letter: "If we live by the Spirit, let us also walk by the Spirit" (5:25). The Spirit is a gift but becomes a duty; in the life of the Christian it is a spiritual aid but also a spiritual obligation. The Spirit delivers us from the power of sin and death and by doing so creates the possibility for us to live in the Spirit. As a condition of our deliverance it is required of us henceforward "that we serve . . . in the new life of the Spirit" (Rom. 7:6) and so make effective the liberty which has been granted to us in the Spirit. Man can also refuse and frustrate the Spirit; man can "grieve the Holy Spirit of God" (Eph. 4:30). The "spiritual man" must live up to the Spirit.

On this point Paul says again and again that the Spirit is received into our hearts (Gal. 4:6; 2 Cor. 1:22); that is to say, the Spirit must be freely willed and accepted. The Spirit is the Holy Spirit, in whom Christians are sanctified: "You were washed, you were sanctified, you were justified in the name of the Lord Jesus Christ and in the Spirit of our God" (1 Cor. 6:11). From this arises the obligation for each one of us to become, and to remain, holy. To neglect this would be to sin against the Holy Spirit. The body is a temple of the Holy Spirit and because it is it must not be polluted (1 Cor. 6:19). The Christian community is the holy temple of God; the Spirit of God dwells in it. If anyone destroys that community which is God's temple, God will destroy him (1 Cor. 3:16f.). Paul, accordingly, gives a stern warning: "God has not called us for uncleanness but in holiness. Therefore whoever disregards this, disregards not man but God, who gives his Holy Spirit to you" (1 Thess. 4:7f.). The gift of the Spirit is not a sort of magical talisman. But "Do not be deceived; God is not mocked. . . . For he who sows to his own flesh will from the flesh reap corruption; but he who sows to the Spirit will from the Spirit reap eternal life" (Gal. 6:7f.). This is something that still holds good for all our dealings and for every day: as the seed is, so will the fruit be—rotten and unusable or sound and good for all eternity. That will become plain to us when we appear before God for judgment.

True, God gives us our beginning and our end. But in between we decide and do things on our own. Although every event in the perpetual conflict between good and evil is foreseen and permitted and used by God, it is also an act in man's life, and for his part in it he will be held responsible. These statements may be difficult to reconcile, but the Christian's faith and religious experience tell him they are true.

Writing to the Christians in Rome, Paul refers with some emotion to the close bond between himself and the community; though many, they are but one body in Christ. Troubled by anxious forebodings with regard to his coming journey to Jerusalem, he asks for their prayers. Are not he and they firmly united to the same Lord by the same charity? "I appeal to you, brethren, by our Lord Jesus Christ and by the love of the Spirit, to strive together with me in your prayers to God on my behalf" (Rom. 15:30). To the Philippians he writes entreatingly: "So if there is any encouragement in Christ, any incentive of love, any participation in the Spirit, any affection and sympathy, complete my joy by being of the same mind, having the same love. . . ." (Phil. 2:1f.).

Christian life, which is life lived in openness and honesty towards God and man, can be described in one word—love. Paul points out that here, too, we are indebted to the Holy

Spirit: "God's love has been poured into our hearts through the Holy Spirit which has been given to us" (Rom. 5:5). The love that Paul is primarily concerned with in this passage is not the good man's love of God but God's love for man. God was the first to move; he turned towards sinful man, taught him virtue, and adopted him as a son. The Christian encounters God's overwhelming love in the Holy Spirit, for God's love pours out the Spirit abundantly upon the Church and upon every individual believer. The Spirit is the intermediary through whom God's love reaches the world. (In St. John's Gospel [14:26; 16:13] the Spirit is the intermediary to whom it is given to complete the work of Christ.) In his Letter to the Colossians (1:8), Paul also alludes to the Christian life as "love in the Spirit." The Church owes its continued existence not to any efforts of its own but to the Spirit whom God has given to it.

It is the Spirit also who transmits the word, the knowledge, and the revelation of God to the Church *as a whole* and to *every one* of its members. "God has revealed to us through the Spirit. For the Spirit searches everything, even the depths of God" (1 Cor. 2:10). Paul applies this to all Christians and not to the apostles only, and his words are equally valid for the Church today. They should not be narrowed down so as to apply only to the official teaching body of the Church, although, of course, the latter has the special charism of teaching. The Spirit knows the depths of God and because of that knowledge distributes his Gifts to all. But what is meant by "the depths of God"? For Paul it means the cross, which shows us clearly that the way to life is through death. Paul says further that all Christians learn this in words not taught by human wisdom but taught by the Spirit (1 Cor.

2:13). Left to himself man could never comprehend God's spiritual message. Only through the Spirit who has been given to him can he understand the word of God (1 Cor. 2:15). Paul then comes to the following conclusion: "The spiritual man judges all things but is himself to be judged by no one" (1 Cor. 2:15). Bold words, indeed, and, moreover, they must be meant to apply to every "spiritual man," and therefore to every Christian. There is no higher court of appeal conceivable than the Spirit of God. The Spirit and those who possess the Spirit are subject to no other standard, whatever worldly wisdom may think. But surely a Christian community—and eventually the whole Church—would be faced with ruin if this or that individual were to press the promptings of the Spirit within him upon the rest of the community, regardless of reasonable restraint? Provided that the Spirit within him really conforms to the law of the Spirit of life in Christ Jesus (Rom. 8:2) and is not a spirit of fanaticism that could disturb or even destroy the community, then the answer to our own question would be this: the individual concerned, being a member of the body of Christ (1 Cor. 12:12–27), has a continuing obligation towards the community and towards the entire Church. All the same, Paul always regards this gift of the Spirit to the community as a means of direct contact with God. Even when he requires obedience he works with them as a servant, for their joy (2 Cor. 1:24).

The Holy Spirit expresses himself in the word of God, in holy writ, which is at the same time a body of doctrine, a profession of belief, and a mass of witness to the truth of that belief. Because all are endowed with the Spirit, all are entitled as of right—are indeed obliged as a duty—to utter the word of God in the Church. Referring to the community as-

sembled for worship, Paul says: "But if all prophesy, and an
unbeliever or outsider enters, he is convicted by all, he is
called to account by all, the secrets of his heart are disclosed;
and so, falling on his face, he will worship God and declare
that God is really among you" (1 Cor. 14:24f.). It necessarily
follows from this universal gift of the Spirit that all Christians
are charged with the duty of proclaiming God's word. The
sole responsibility for doing so does not rest on the official
liturgist, the priest at the altar. The liturgy, therefore, is ade-
quately celebrated only when all join in its recital; only then
will it carry conviction. Paul also expressly concedes to women
the right to proclaim the word; but the woman, when she
prays or "prophesies," must have her head veiled: "Any
woman who prays or prophesies with her head unveiled dishonors her head" (1 Cor. 11:5). In saying this he only
endorses the custom current in his day whereby respectable
Jewish and Greek women wore a veil in public as a mark of
decency and decorum. But the main thing is that women
have the right to bear witness in Christian worship. This must
always be borne in mind when the following passage in the
same letter is adduced to the contrary: "The women should
keep silence in the churches. . . . If there is anything they
desire to know, let them ask their husbands at home" (1 Cor.
14:34f.). Perhaps both rules can be reconciled by saying that,
while women have the right to speak the word of God in
the assembly, they should not disturb the good order of the
gathering with questions and disputes about profane matters,
which should be discussed at home. When assembled for
worship the Church must bear witness, and so Paul exhorts
the Ephesians to "be filled with the Spirit, addressing one
another in psalms and hymns and spiritual songs, singing and

making melody to the Lord with all your heart, always and for everything giving thanks [literally 'eucharist'] in the name of our Lord Jesus Christ to God the Father" (5:18f.).

The Church is the fellowship of the Spirit and Paul specially stresses that the Church's mission sanctifies the world through the Holy Spirit. He tells the Christians in Rome he is writing to them "because of the grace given me by God to be a minister of Christ Jesus to the Gentiles in the priestly service of the gospel of God, so that the offering of the Gentiles may be acceptable, sanctified by the Holy Spirit" (15:15f.). Paul is not just a teacher here in this world; he is a priest as well, mediating God's grace and salvation to the world. The peoples of the world will be saved through the word of God in the gospel; through the sacraments, which are signs made by the mighty finger of God; but also and always through the faith of those who hear and heed God's word and prize the sacraments which bring him to themselves. All this comes about through the power of the Spirit who is active always and everywhere.

Freedom and life for all in the Spirit

"The Lord is the Spirit, and where the Spirit of the Lord is, there is freedom." This pithy sentence occurs in Paul's Second Letter to the Corinthians (3:17). But how can he call our Lord Jesus Christ the Spirit?

We have an entirely inadequate idea of the presence of Christ if we think of it as simply a remembrance, something merely present in the memory, just as bygone generations may be present in the memories of an admiring and grateful posterity. Christ's presence can, of course, be recalled as the holy and heroic exemplar of faith in God and obedience to God's will; saints and other holy people are present in this way in our spiritual tradition. And the teaching of Christ in holy writ may also be said to bring him to us. But the presence of Christ is far more than all this.

Christ is always present as the almighty, living, active Spirit. As such he is the integrity and sanctity, life and fullness of the Church. He works wonders on those who listen to him and on those who want to hear him. To be his disciple is to know the living Lord in his Spirit, to receive and entertain him, and to submit to his sweet yoke. Christ is "one spirit with the Lord" (1 Cor. 6:17).

"Where the Spirit of the Lord is, there is freedom" (2 Cor. 3:17). The Spirit is freedom from the Old Law and freedom, therefore, from the weakness of the flesh, from sin and death. The Spirit frees from the letter that cramps and confines; the Spirit opens up the possibility of love. But liberty should not be mistaken for licence. It was not long, indeed, before the liberty preached by Paul came to be misinterpreted in this sense, and he had to warn a Christian community that liberation from the Old Law did not mean licence to reject God's commandments; it meant freedom in the service of God and one's neighbor (Rom. 6:1,15,22). The granting of this freedom in the Church should not be lost sight of or held in check. Supernatural faith has a freedom and immediacy before God which must always be respected by human authority. Freedom, also, is a virtue, and faith and love have no need to recoil from it in alarm. It is the inner assent and acceptance that count and not the command from outside. Lip-service is no longer good enough; faith must be heartfelt. Let us have a little more confidence in God's generosity in the bestowal of his Spirit.

St. Paul teaches us that the Spirit is given to the Church as a whole and to every member of it. The Church was founded by the Holy Spirit and is a fellowship of the Holy Spirit (2 Cor. 13:13). It is "one body and one Spirit" (Eph. 4:4). Every member of it, therefore, is included in the wish of the apostle, which is also a promise: "May the God of hope fill you with all joy and peace in believing, so that by the power of the Holy Spirit you may abound in hope" (Rom. 15:13). Paul takes words and ideas from the Old and New

Testaments relating to the Spirit and links them together in a precious chain: hope, joy, peace, faith, power and spirit. God is the God of hope, and fulfillment is guaranteed by his own infinite truth and faithfulness. He has revealed the future in holy writ, which is his word. As an earnest of salvation in store he gives the Church present peace and joy. And peace and joy will continue to bless the Faith and every human decision and deed which accords with the Faith. God bestows all his gifts through the medium of his Spirit in whose hands he leaves everything. Every good deed is a manifestation of the power and influence of the Spirit in the Church.

In his Letter to the Romans Paul ranges widely over the Christian life and goes deeper and deeper into the theology of this "life in the Spirit" (Rom. 8:1–17). His words will continue to bring consolation to every Christian until the end of time.

Paul compares the Old with the New Testament: "There is therefore now no condemnation for those who are in Christ Jesus. For the law of the Spirit of life in Christ Jesus has set me free from the law of sin and death" (Rom. 8:1f.), which the law of the Old Testament had not within itself the power to do. While it impressed man's obligations upon him, the result was only to make the transgressor all too conscious of his inability to live up to them. It did not set him a step farther on the path of righteousness. It was a law that could only beget condemnation and death (Rom. 7:5,13). Now, however, it has been overridden and replaced by a new dispensation, the dispensation of redemption and salvation. True, this new dispensation enforces obligations of its own. The Spirit is not a sort of vague, aimless, unregulated enthusiasm. The Spirit acts in accordance with his own divine economy. But law and liberty are not opposites, and the Spirit tends rather towards liberty. He is the bringer of life, the new, meaningful life of the present as well as the future life. Again we see that the Spirit has nothing to do with unbridled enthusiasm or anything of that sort; the Spirit is given in and through Christ Jesus to the Christian who heeds the word of his Lord and steadfastly believes that God's plan for man's salvation was fulfilled in Christ. And if the Spirit is bestowed in Christ, then it must be bestowed within the community which is truly and exclusively his, that is, within the Church. Only in such circumstances is true liberty attained; otherwise man simply shuts himself up in a prison of his own making.

"For those who live according to the flesh set their minds on the things of the flesh, but those who live according to the Spirit set their minds on the things of the Spirit" (Rom. 8:15). The antagonism between sin-and-death and spirit-and-life can also be described as the antagonism between flesh and spirit. By "flesh" Paul never means sins of the flesh in the narrowest sense, that is, impurity. He refers rather to man in his natural state enslaved by sin from the beginning, man against God and, therefore, man to whom everything is of no avail. The "spirit" as opposed to the "flesh" is the Spirit of God and all that he brings about; the fruit he produces in time is good for eternity. The fleshly man leads a fleshly life. Only those who have received the Spirit can live according to the Spirit; life in the Spirit is not the result of simple goodwill but of the new creation in the Spirit, and the new creation in the Spirit is God's work of salvation for us which is antecedent to all goodwill.

"To set the mind on the flesh is death, but to set the

mind on the Spirit is life and peace" (Rom. 8:6). Left to his own unaided natural powers, man always peters out in futility and death. In his struggle to advance himself he may use many methods; he may go after wealth and power, sublimate his emotions in fanatical devotion to his daily work, train and exercise his intellect, and even cultivate and practise virtue. But the sad truth is that in the long run all his efforts come to naught; they all end in futility and death. Only through the divine gift of the Spirit is true life to be found, and that peace which the divine economy of salvation plans for us all.

"But you are not in the flesh, you are in the Spirit, if the Spirit of God really dwells in you. Any one who does not have the Spirit of Christ does not belong to him" (Rom. 8:9). Paul reminds the Roman Christians of the complete transformation that has been brought about by God's action in redeeming them and sending them his Spirit. Being redeemed, they are no longer "in the flesh." He knew, of course, that they were still capable of committing sin. In all his letters to the young churches he is aware that sin and error are to be found in their midst as well as anywhere else. But in their case, nevertheless, something decisive has happened. God has intervened. The Church has received the Spirit of God. From now on all who remain true to the Christian faith will be able to live according to the Spirit.

"But if Christ is in you, although your bodies are dead because of sin, your spirits are alive because of righteousness" (Rom. 8:10). The new creation means that what Christ achieved by his death and resurrection is granted to all Christians. By dying he passed judgment on sin, and not only deprived it of its power but did away with it forever. And, insofar as they are the result of sin, man's mortal body and his natural, human life are done away with, too. Man can now really and truly live according to God's Spirit and God's justice because both have been bestowed on him.

"If the Spirit of him who raised Jesus from the dead dwells in you, he who raised Christ Jesus from the dead will give life to your mortal bodies also through his Spirit which dwells in you" (Rom. 8:11). The full meaning of true life will henceforth be plain to all. True life will apply to the body as well as to the soul. The body, indeed, is mortal and its mortality is, and remains, the badge of man's fall, of man's sin. But Christ's body has been put to death on account of man's sin and with it the body of every Christian. Christ, too, has risen from the dead, and he who raised Christ from the dead will also raise the Christian from the dead. This will be effected through the Spirit who does God's work in this world. The Spirit that is said by Paul to conquer death is not the human spirit, the immortal spirit which is our soul; death was conquered by God's actual work of salvation carried out through his Spirit. The God who, by Christ's resurrection, made death powerless, completes his work when, through the Spirit of the new creation, he delivers man from the bondage of his mortality and endows him with eternal life.

"If you live according to the flesh you will die, but if by the Spirit you put to death the deeds of the body, you will live" (Rom. 8:13). The decision that the Christian is called upon to make has irrevocable results. He opts for death or for life. Life according to the flesh profits him nothing and ends in death; life according to the Spirit wins for him eternal life.

"For all who are led by the Spirit of God are sons of God" (Rom. 8:14). The Spirit makes us children of God. As God's Spirit he brings man into harmony with God. Those who let themselves be guided by the Spirit think as God thinks and will what he wills. They will resemble God as children resemble their father. And children are heirs (Rom. 8:17). If God is life, they as children of God will possess life.

"For you did not receive the spirit of slavery to fall back into fear, but you have received the spirit of sonship, in virtue of which we cry, 'Abba! Father!' " (Rom. 8:15). To be a son is certainly the very reverse of being a slave. Under the Old Law which only begot sin and fear of punishment a state of slavery had prevailed. Now the Law is obsolete. The Christian is no longer the slave but the son of God, and he proves it by addressing God as "Father" in his prayer. Paul was, of course, thinking of the prayer which our Lord had taught the disciples, the "Lord's Prayer." Only a son has the right to pray like that.

"The Spirit himself bears witness with our spirit that we are children of God" (Rom. 8:16). None of us, sinful creatures that we are, have an inherent right to address the almighty, all-holy God as "Father." To do so would be the height of impudence, let alone presumption. But Paul and every other Christian know that the worshipper does not do so on his own initiative. When the Christian addresses God as "Father" the Spirit of God who dwells within him joins in his prayer. When the Christian prays, his prayer is not merely that of one human being. For the Spirit who prays with him is the Spirit who fills the whole Church, the Spirit who moves many other hearts to pray. This communion of prayer bears witness to their common knowledge that they are children of God. All members of the Church can rest assured that they are really and truly children of God.

The spiritual priesthood of all Christians

St. John the Evangelist, like St. Paul, has much to tell us about the Holy Spirit. Indeed he is, in a very special sense, the Apostle of the Spirit. He develops the theology of the new reality of the Spirit to such a degree that the stupendous power and effect of the Spirit are put beyond further question.

A well-known passage in St. John's Gospel refers to the man who lives according to the Spirit. In this passage the evangelist makes use of the two meanings of the Greek word *pneuma*, as of the Hebrew *ruah*, "wind" and "spirit." "The wind [spirit] blows where it wills, and you hear the sound of it, but you do not know whence it comes or whither it goes; so it is with every one who is born of the Spirit" (Jn. 8:8). The wind is something that still eludes the understanding of most of us. It comes and goes mysteriously, but its existence cannot be denied; we hear its sound and see its effects. The Spirit, too, eludes us. The Spirit is hidden from the world, invisible, but nevertheless a tremendous reality. There are men in the world who are "born of the Spirit," live according to the Spirit, who are men of a new creation. They also are hidden from the

world. They are not identifiable by miracles or marvels. There
is nothing to distinguish them from anyone else. We do not
know whence they come or wither they go. We do not even
know who they are, and even if we did we could not look into
their hearts.

St. John's Gospel, in common with the rest of the New
Testament, contrasts the "flesh" and the "spirit." "It is the
spirit that gives life" (Jn. 6:63). To the flesh belongs what is
earthly and worldly and to the spirit all that is other-worldly,
holy, divine. Man can choose between these two possibilities
of flesh and spirit. But he may not choose between them in-
differently; his freedom of choice is qualified. The "either-or"
with which man is confronted is—at least to begin with—not
an "either-or" of his own will but one determined from
outside and put to him. And its source can only be the new
creation which God has brought into being through the medium of the Spirit. For Christ says, "Unless one is born of
water and the Spirit he cannot enter the kingdom of God"
(Jn. 3:5). Here the Gospel obviously refers to the sacrament
of baptism, which, at the time John was writing, had already
been in use in the Church for a long time. But, while the
sacrament is indeed the foundation of the Christian life, it is
not to be regarded as a purely external, quasi-magical ritual;
it is a vehicle of the Spirit and is effective only if received in
the Spirit. Both together, water and Spirit, constitute the
sacrament.

St. John's Gospel speaks in similar terms of the other great
sacrament, the Eucharist. True, Christ says, "He who eats
my flesh and drinks my blood has eternal life" (Jn. 6:54), and
so Christ's flesh is really eaten and his blood really drunk in

this sacrament. But later Christ says, "It is the spirit that
gives life, the flesh is of no avail" (Jn. 6:63).

God's gift of the Spirit would have no meaning for those
who think and act only in terms of the flesh; they would be
in no position to receive him and open their hearts to his
influence. And it is God's Spirit and only God's Spirit that
makes the divine plan of salvation effective in the hearts of
men.

The only true worshippers, therefore, are those who worship "in spirit and truth" (Jn. 4:23). The two words and
ideas of this much-quoted phrase would be misunderstood if
they were taken to mean "in spirit and truth as interpreted
by contemporary thought." The sentence that contains them
is not a philosophical judgment implying, let us say, that
God's being is invisible and immaterial in the sense that it is
not composed of matter. If it were a philosophical judgment,
God's being would be describable in terms of philosophy's
current views on what spirit is. The New Testament, (however, is more than philosophy: it is the word of God revealed
to man. The word and idea of "spirit" must accordingly be
understood in the sense in which they are used in St. John's
Gospel and the rest of the New Testament. There "worship
in spirit" means more than an inner, spiritual worship of God
(as against, perhaps, a religion that practises a visible cult or
is tied to definite places of worship). Similarly, truth means
more than knowledge of God refined by intellectual insight.
"Spirit" in the New Testament means the divine Spirit bestowed on men by God, and "truth" means God's word
revealed by Christ and God's truth incarnate in Christ. Christ
is "the way, and the truth, and the life" (Jn. 14:6). To know
the truth means to know the true God in Christ whom God

has sent (Jn. 17:3). Worship, in its fullness, is worship paid to God in accord with his word, and in the community which is the creation of the Spirit. True worshippers of God are born of the Spirit and taught by the Spirit, for this Spirit is the "Spirit of truth" (Jn. 14:17; 15:26). He will teach Christ's disciples all things, bringing to their mind at the same time all that Jesus had told them. He will teach them to understand the gospel of their divine Master and to preach it to the peoples of the earth. "The Spirit . . . will bear witness to me; and you also are witnesses. . . ." (Jn. 15:26). The power of the Spirit is behind the Church's knowledge of the truth and her preaching of it. The Spirit "will guide you [the disciples] into all the truth" (Jn. 16:13). Truth, then, means God's revelation. Thanks to the power of the Spirit which has been given them, Christians feel confident that, however dark and uncertain the future, God's word and revelation will always shine through. In the light of God's word, too, the Christian will interpret the present. In all this the Spirit of truth will be the Church's all-powerful helper and counsellor (Jn. 14:16,26; 15:26; 16:7). Because of this the Holy Spirit or Holy Ghost has long been known throughout Christendom as the Comforter.

The Spirit is bestowed upon the Church in superabundance. "It is not by measure that he [God] gives the Spirit" (Jn. 3:34). And again, " 'Out of his [Christ's] heart shall flow rivers of living water.' Now this he [Jesus] said about the Spirit which those who believed in him were to receive" (Jn. 7:38f.). The Spirit will be poured out by the infinitely generous hand of God's bounty. In the power of the Spirit sin will be blotted out forever. On Easter evening Christ breathed on his disciples and said to them, "Receive the Holy Spirit. If you forgive

the sins of any, they are forgiven" (Jn. 20:22f.). But the Spirit
is given to every Christian as well as to the Church: "By this
we know that we abide in him and he in us, because he has
given us of his own Spirit" (1 Jn. 4:13).

The Church is often referred to in the New Testament as
the house of God built by God, Christ and the Spirit. Thus
in Paul's Letter to the Ephesians (2:21f.) it is called "a holy
temple in the Lord" and "a dwelling place of God in the
Spirit." The Church exists by virtue of, and in, the Spirit. It
is built as a "spiritual house" for a holy priesthood (1 Pet.
2:5). It is contrasted with the temple of the Old Covenant
which was an earthly temple built of stone; the new house of
God is filled with the Spirit, is indeed built by the Spirit. Not
by the good will of men or the virtue of good men is the
Church built, but by the Spirit as he goes about his work of
re-creation here on earth, in accordance with the divine plan
of salvation. In the Letter last quoted Peter concludes that all
members of the Church, being each endowed with the Spirit,
form "a royal priesthood" (1 Pet. 2:9). "Royal" implies freedom and independence, and "priesthood" the function of
preaching the gospel, the honor of personal service at the altar
and of offering the sacrifice that is so effective a medium for
transmitting God's grace to the world. Peter says so expressly:
"You are . . . God's own people that you may declare the
wonderful deeds of him who called you out of darkness into
his marvellous light" (1 Pet. 2:9); they are "a holy priesthood,
to offer spiritual sacrifices acceptable to God through Jesus
Christ" (1 Pet. 2:5). The more refined idea of sacrifice—not
altogether unknown even among the heathen—is particularly
evident in the Old and New Testaments. It placed no value
on the offering of material gifts as such; they were most

efficacious when they expressed in some way the spirit in which the sacrifice was offered, the will behind it. The Christian sacrifice can only be a spiritual sacrifice. It is most pleasing to God, for it is offered in union with the high priest, Christ, and it is a sacrifice in accordance with the Spirit who has been given to the Church. But although it is called a spiritual sacrifice, it is far from being a purely figurative or unreal sacrifice. For the Holy Spirit is a divine reality, and the reality of God is the most compelling of all realities, incomparably superior to all human and earthly reality.

The words "spirit" and "spiritual" occur again and again throughout the New Testament. In a few places "spirit" means the human spirit (as in Mt. 26:41; Mk. 2:8; 1 Cor. 2:11; 1 Thess. 5:23). In the vast majority of cases, however, it stands for the divine Spirit, the Spirit of God. In reading and interpreting the New Testament, therefore, we always take these words to refer primarily to the Holy Spirit except where it is obvious that they do not.

In a few New Testament passages we can discern the source of what was to be our doctrine of the Holy Spirit as a person of the Blessed Trinity (Mt. 28:19; Jn. 14:26; 2 Cor. 13:14; 1 Pet. 1:2). The Holy Spirit is most often conceived and depicted as God in powerful action. The whole idea of the Spirit and the words used to express it imply the life-giving, sanctifying power of the presence of God (Mt. 12:28; Rom. 5:5; 1 Cor. 2:10, 6:11) and of Christ (Jn. 6:63; Rom. 8:9; 2 Cor. 3:17) in the world, in the Church, and in each member of the Church (1 Cor. 12:13; Eph. 4:4; 1 Pet. 2:5). The Spirit is power: "You shall receive power when the Holy Spirit has come upon you" (Acts 1:8).

The Spirit is also the driving force that urges the Christian on to perfection, and an earnest of the good things in store (Rom. 8:23; 14:17; 1 Cor. 15:44–7; Gal. 6:8; 2 Cor. 1:22; 5:5). When he takes up his abode in the heart of the true believer he gives his host a foretaste of the world to come and an increase of faith in it, and guarantees that God will bring it to fulfillment in the end. Meanwhile the Church moves by the light of faith towards her distant goal and the Spirit lifts man out of the mire of earthly and sinful things, spiritualizing man's body, life and nature so that they may be fit eventually to enter into God's glory. On the way, faith and love strain their eyes to get a glimpse of the beloved: "The Spirit and the Bride say 'Come' . . . Come, Lord Jesus!" (Rev. 12:17,20). The bride is the Church, who lives in the Spirit of God. But she is also the whole world, which is filled with the creator spirit. The Spirit presses and yearns for the fulfillment which Christ's second coming will bring.

The Old Testament looked forward with intense longing to the distant day of salvation: "Would that all the Lord's people were prophets, that the Lord would put his spirit upon them!" (Num. 11:29). In the Church of the new People of God that longing is satisfied at last, and the fulfillment of God's promise has begun. And so Paul writes to his young churches: "Do not quench the Spirit" (1 Thess. 5:19); "Be filled with the Spirit" (Eph. 5:18).

Now and then, perhaps, impatient or depressed on account of what seems to us the weakness and slowness of the Spirit's action today in the Church and in our own hearts, we may be tempted to ask whether this is the same Spirit who came down in a rush of wind and a blaze of fire on the disciples at Pentecost. The Old Testament story of Elijah may well give us the answer. The prophet, despairing of success in his prophetic mission, hid himself in a cave on Mount Horeb and longed to die. Then he heard a voice that told him to go out and stand on the mountain in the presence of the Lord: "And behold . . . a great and strong wind rent the mountains and broke in pieces the rocks . . . but the Lord was not in the wind; and after the wind an earthquake, but the Lord was not in the earthquake; and after the earthquake a fire, but the Lord was not in the fire; and after the fire a still small voice. And when Elijah heard it, he wrapped his face in his mantle and went out and stood at the entrance of the cave." Then the Lord went by. " 'What are you doing here, Elijah?' " The prophet told his pitiful tale. "And the Lord said to him: 'Go, return on your way' " (1 Kgs. 19).

The action of the Spirit is not always like the rush of a mighty wind. It may be only a breath of air, a mere whisper. But even so it can fill the Church; it can fill the whole world. And the still small voice may whisper to us also: "Go, return on your way."

Notes

1. *The Holy Bible, Revised Standard Version,* New York, Nelson, 1946, 1952. All scriptural quotations in this book are from this version, copyrighted 1946 and 1952 by the Division of Christian Education of the National Council of Churches.

2 CHANGES IN CHRISTIAN SPIRITUALITY

by Thomas Sartory

TRANSLATED BY FRED D. WIECK

Introduction

It takes no little courage to write on "Changes in Christian Spirituality." "Spirituality" has become a fashionable word these days; but "to refuse to employ fashionable words means to withdraw from the present."[1] Anyone writing on spirituality becomes involved willy-nilly in the current controversies among Catholic theologians. (We need only recall the altercations surrounding the publication of Louis Bouyer's *Introduction to the Spiritual Life.*) Since spirituality "today means either the spiritual life as a living experience, or the scientific study of the spiritual life,"[2] any discussion of it assumes at once a subjective character, and consequently a certain tenor. To some readers, the way in which the author lays his stresses may seem helpful, while others may look in vain for their personal experience of God and Christ. For example, there are those who agree with Sudbrack's view that "we, too, can encounter the Lord in no other way (!) than through the word of Scripture, in which the preaching of the apostles has found its valid formulation passed on to us by the Church; and through his sacramental presence which achieves its most concentrated form in baptism and the Eucharist"; they agree further that "originally, the sacramental life was properly speaking the whole life of a Christian," and that Christian spirituality is impoverished when it loses its living relationship with dogma, sacrament, and the facts of salvation. Such readers will no doubt feel disappointed because they will find in the following pages no explicit mention of dogmas, baptism, the Eucharist, and the other sacraments. But that omission does not reflect a specific intention. If in the reflections that follow we concentrate on the living Spirit of God which pervades the entire life of a Christian in the world, and which is the Spirit of Christ (just as the name and substance of Christian *spirituality* suggest), we do not mean to deny the way in which the exalted Lord works in the sacraments or in the Church. We only intend to set out for distant shores that in the past have all too often lain below the horizon, and on which today more than ever settlements are being established by committed Christians who have consciously shaped their existence to conform with the modern changes of the worldly scene. There are indeed many Christians to whom the sacramental life no longer means the Christian's *whole* life, and for whom the "Marian character of all Christian spirituality" (Sudbrack, Hans Urs von Balthasar, and others) is no longer the beginning and the end.

Nothing is further from my mind than the assertion that the spotlights I set up represent the only light. I only mean to illuminate certain long-forgotten aspects, in order to show clearly the change in the Christian life which is in fact taking place today. Let no one suppose that I despise and reject anything not explicitly mentioned in these pages—they are not meant to be anything like a *summa* of Christian spirituality.

Once again, I express the hope that my readers will share their thoughts with me, and engage me in a critical dialogue. It will help me to come properly to grips with the matter in hand.

What does Christ want?

Are we today undergoing a *reform* of Christian spirituality? The more I ponder the question, the more I find myself objecting to the word "reform." There is of course much talk today about reforms in the Church, and there are doubtless many areas where reforms can and must be planned and executed. It is as easy to imagine a reform of the liturgy as of the Curia. But a "reform" of Christian spirituality? There are certain things that will not let themselves be managed so easily by human planning, arrangements, or reforms. Can man construct a friendship, or reform a marriage? Clearly there are areas in life that are *sui generis*, where human planning, manipulation, and "engineering" are strictly limited, because these areas include much that grows and thrives and flowers, or else withers away and perishes, according to its own laws. "Love knows no laws," we say. There are many things that know no laws, that simply cannot be shaped at will, or reformed according to plan.

One of these things is what we call "Christian spirituality." This will surprise no one who is in the least aware that Christian spirituality has something to do with the *spiritus sanctus*, the Holy Spirit, the divine Spirit. The Spirit is the *spiritus rector* in which a Christian thinks, speaks and acts wholly as Christian. If indeed there is such a thing as a reform of Christian spirituality, the initiative for it can lie only with God, not with man.

Accordingly, man tends to feel here subjectively that something is happening to him, rather than that he is doing something himself—that here "something" takes place, "something" is changing. And the *new thing* seems to be rising from such depths, and in such elemental, radical ways, that we may feel caught up, with or against our will, in a change whose true dimensions we cannot yet fathom. Hence I prefer to speak of a *change* of Christian spirituality rather than a reform.

But what does spirituality mean? Is spirituality to take the place of a "piety" that has become a little suspect? Or is spirituality merely a fancy word for our old friend, the "spiritual" life? The word can be used in the widest sense—there is no reason why we cannot speak of Buddhist or Hindu spirituality. But we are here concerned with *Christian* spirituality. Accordingly we use the term in the narrower sense given to it automatically by the French, who hear the echo of *Saint esprit* whenever the word *spiritualité* is pronounced; we, too, intend the words "spiritual life" to refer not to just any lofty spirit, but to that divine power which is called *pneuma*, Spirit, in the New Testament. We must remember this terminology, so useful to biblical scholars and theologians. In keeping with general practice, the word "spiritual" is used where Paul for the same reason uses the word "pneumatic."[3]

What is the spiritual life of a Christian like? Or rather,

what ought it to be like if it really corresponded to the Christian vocation? Hans Urs von Balthasar lists exceedingly strict criteria. To him, the *quintessence* of Christian existence consists in the basic attitude of "leaving everything"—leaving everything so that we may be totally submerged in radical surrender to God. "The inner meaning of the Gospel demands that man imitate Jesus in such a way that he stakes everything ultimately on this one card, abandoning the rest of the pack. He must leave everything, without looking back, without trying to create a synthesis between Jesus and leaving one's home, between Jesus and burying one's father. . . ."[4] Balthasar's formulation is intentionally extreme, not to say austere, in order to bring out the spirituality which, in his view, is alone in keeping with the gospel; it is not surprising, then, that for him only the "saints" (canonized or not) are *real* Christians —while all others are ultimately "compromisers" whose existence is "justified" only by the existence of the saints. In his view, a legitimate Christian synthesis of Christ and the world, Christian and worldly existence, is an impossibility. It is thus logical for Balthasar to see the purest expression of the spirituality of the universal Church in the spirituality of the secular institutes: chastity, poverty, and obedience are for him modalities of the love which renounces and *thereby* redeems, the love which from the beginning—and long before secular institutes and religious orders ever existed—has constituted the general spirit of Christlike love within the Church.[5] His entire essay is inspired by an impressive rejection of all compromise. This much must be admitted. And indeed, there is no getting around the plain fact that Christ himself was without compromise. Still, in considering *what* Christ demanded and *how* he demanded it, we must not lose sight of the circumstances in which he demanded it. To *leave* one's wife, child, father, mother, house and belongings is by no means meritorious in itself, either morally or "religiously" (and Balthasar would not claim that it is); nor is it in any absolute sense better or "more perfect." Christ, as the Gospels show, did not in the least expect this renunciation from everyone who had accepted his word. Those, of course, who were to follow him as disciples on his journeys through Judea and Galilee could not at the same time stay with their families. That goes without saying. In this sense Christ insisted on a clearcut decision. He had no use for disciples who were half-hearted, not totally engaged; who remained involved in the worries and petty cares of what they necessarily had to leave behind them.

There is no doubt that much of what Christ demanded of his disciples must be understood primarily in the light of their very concrete situation, because the disciples could not in actual fact roam the country with the Master and at the same time stay at home among their families. But does this reminder—that some of Christ's words to his disciples are dictated by the concrete situation—mean that we of a later age are no longer concerned with the call to make an uncompromising decision? No. Nothing in the Gospels is so totally time-bound. Nor would the evangelists have handed on Christ's words about discipleship if they had not been convinced that those words had a claim to make even on the community after the Pasch. At the same time, it can be shown from the Epistles and Acts that the community of the Pasch by no means understood Christ's call to follow him as a general command to "leave everything." Peter, for instance, went home to his wife after Christ's departure, and later took her

with him on his missions; the other apostles, too, took their
wives along (cf. 1 Cor. 9:5).

To leave everything, give up everything, renounce everything seems very heroic. But many an "heroic" action can be
immoral—if it is inhuman. The question is: for what purpose?
Christ's demand does not in essence require a supremely radical readiness to renounce because only such readiness would
make a radical surrender to God possible: rather, it calls for a
supremely radical *readiness for commitment* to the "cause" of
the kingdom of God. Obviously, when it comes to God's
kingship of the world, which begins with Christ, everything
else must stand aside, not just our home and property but
even our own family. Here, it holds true that no one is worthy
of Christ who places his own concern above his responsibility
for the cause of the kingdom of God. Here, those who have
staked their bet "on Christ's card" are put to the test: have
they confidence that *God's* kingdom in the world is worth
the risk of *everything?* "Do not be anxious about tomorrow,
for tomorrow will be anxious for itself. But seek first his kingdom and his righteousness, and all these things shall be yours
as well" (Mt. 6:34,33). The man who follows Christ, then,
should be totally ready for God and God's kingdom, unim-
peded by worldly worries—not in order to leave the world, as
did the Essenes and the Qumran community, but rather in
order to do God's will in every instance, without compromise:
"Whoever does the will of God is my brother, and sister, and
mother" (Mk. 3:36).

Now this is precisely the point where there is emerging
today a radical return to the original Christian spirituality. For
centuries the kingdom of God has been conceived as a reality
purely of the beyond, as the "kingdom in heaven" where the

soul goes after death, and not the kingdom of God which has invaded even this present moment. An assured place in "heaven" became a widespread motivation for the radical renunciation of the "world." In this sense, the basic attitude remained egocentric, an overwhelming anxiousness for one's own self—the very anxiousness from which Christ's call is meant to deliver man. Christ demands that man be so totally concerned with the cause of God's kingdom in the world that his concern for himself and his belongings fades by comparison. Christ is concerned not with "heaven" but with the "world," God's kingdom in the world: that "his kingdom come," and that his will be done on "earth" as it is in "heaven." Christ takes this position neither with the appetites of the libertine and worldling which constantly tempt every man, nor with the ascetic's unconditional flight from the world, as the ascetic John practised it, but in between. Christ wants neither subjection *to* nor a rejection *of* the world, but the surrender *in* the world to God and thus to mankind. (Concerning the world-related character of the Christian message, see especially the Gospel according to Luke.)

First seek the kingdom of God and his righteousness? Of course—but where, and how? God's dominion is not a Platonic idea, nor is the justice and righteousness under his sway an abstraction. The Bible, in its unity of Old and New Testaments, knows that "God's kingdom" is wherever there is peace and justice among men, where their common life is ruled by brotherly solidarity, where no man is oppressed and despised. And Christ demands precisely that man *in* the world be free of the *malice* of the world, always ready for God and for God's claim as he encounters it in his fellow men in the world's daily life.

In the light of a theology of God's kingdom that is in keeping with the Gospels, Hans Urs von Balthasar's assertion—that there can be no legitimate synthesis of Christ and the world, Christian existence and existence in the world—would seem untenable. We need not be surprised, therefore, that Balthasar's essay in *Concilium* from which we have quoted is followed immediately, in the same issue, by an article entitled "The Lines of Force in the Spiritual Currents of Our Time," in which the Dominican Albert-Marie Besnard advances a totally opposite view. According to Besnard, any spirituality that is guided by the core of Christ's message—the kingdom of God which is about to begin—must necessarily be world-oriented.

The Christian of today, Besnard points out, is above all looking for a spirituality of the things that make up his daily workaday life. He is asking for a spirituality of married life, work, human encounter, leisure, and so on, and imbuing these areas and relationships with the color of a "spiritual intention" (such as the "good intention" to do everything "for the greater glory of God") is not in the least what he is concerned with. Today's Christian, says Besnard, understands, by the "spiritualization" of his life, something totally different from—for example—the interruption of his daily work by brief pauses for reflection on "God," so that in the midst of his hopes and anxieties a special area is reserved for a generalized relationship with God. This kind of "spiritual" life is simply unacceptable to the Christian of our time. Just let us recall a typical feature of the older spirituality: the faithful were enjoined to keep their workday holy, oriented to God by the frequent prayers, however brief, which would redirect their hearts to him. "Ejaculatory prayer," this exercise in piety was called.

The structural change of Christian spirituality today consists above all in this—that the spiritual life is no longer identified with the religious life. The various forms in which the religious life is realized no longer constitute the whole of the spiritual life, but have only a service function within it. Prayer does not thereby become "superfluous" (we shall return to this point), but its position in the whole of the spiritual life is given an entirely new value.

The spiritual life is life itself—life "in the world," to the extent to which it is lived in a *Christian* manner, in the Spirit of Christ, the Spirit of God. In his Letter to the Galatians, Paul gives a hint of the responses and attitudes that determine a man in whose life the Holy Spirit is operative. What Paul calls the "fruits" of the Spirit have no necessary connection with the religious life; they can manifest themselves in the everyday life of the world. Indeed, even more than in the life of the cloister, the love, joy, peace, patience, kindness, goodness, faithfulness, gentleness and self-control which Paul describes are needed in all our daily contacts in the world. In Colossians 2:23, St. Paul even opposes false asceticism and arbitrary self-mortification explicitly: "These have indeed an appearance of wisdom in promoting rigor of devotion and self-abasement and severity to the body, but they are of no value, serving only to indulge the flesh." The apostle is convinced that this voluntary asceticism can be practised to feed spiritual arrogance and so produce a "fleshly" attitude of mind.

If we just take the concept of the "spiritual life" literally,

it means nothing other than "life in the Spirit"—and at once
the idea bursts out of the confines of formal religious life. For,
according to the New Testament, life reaches its fullness
through the Holy Spirit when it is lived according to the
spirit of Christ, above all in fraternal love.

Divine service in the world

The central importance given to brotherly love in the New Testament shows clearly how little the Christian spiritual life can be conceived in terms of so-called religious exercises. "He who abides in love abides in God," we read in 1 John 4:16, "and God abides in him." John draws this conclusion from the decisive principle that God, in his essential nature, is love, and that love—genuine love—is therefore a reflection of the divine mode of being. And the thing in man that is from God, and thus renders man capable of love, is God's Spirit. We must take these words in their most concrete and most real sense. For we are dealing here with something actual and real, and only that is actually real which is active, which acts. The First Epistle of John asks matter-of-factly: "If anyone has the world's goods and sees his brother in need, yet closes his heart against him, how does God's love abide in him?" (3:17). A man who does not love has nothing in him of God's ways, he has not been "begotten of God" (as John puts it in his symbolic language), does not have God for his father, in him God's "seed" is not alive and active. In 1 John 3:9, God's

Spirit in the children of God is actually called the *sperma*, the seed of God: God's nature in man's nature, which makes man resemble God and so makes him one who loves. "He who abides in love abides in God, and God abides in him!"

Faith in the Holy Spirit is therefore the faith that God is in man, that the divine nature is active in man, that man, having God for his father, is recognizable because he loves like God. As soon as this is said, we note, very different categories apply from the accustomed categories of "religion." One does not have to go to church to encounter God, and one's soul can have union with God before a prayer is said. Our usual practice of calling the church building the "house of God" could mislead us. "Do you not know," Paul asks the Corinthians, "that your body is a temple of the Holy Spirit within you, which you have from God?" (1 Cor. 6:19). After this, what sense would there be in setting up a barrier between a sacred and a profane realm, between the area of the spiritual and the area of the worldly life?

A mother of eight wrote to me: "Since I no longer live alone, but am married and have children, a totally new feeling for community is growing in me. To live together, eat together, sleep under one roof together—all these forms of community have become necessities of life for me in an altogether unique way. The joy of experiencing community in marriage prompted us from the start to gather friends around us with whom we had something in common, so that we can have conversations with them, and be together in a way that each is there for the others. . . . We have found that such being together gives us sustenance, and none of us can any longer do without this food, because each of us has come to take a part in a 'life' which first made life lovable and put a

new joy into it. . . . After this and similar experiences, there
came what you call the removal of the frontiers of the sacred.
The day-to-day natural life became the true reality. We had
experiences of God in places where before we would never
have dared expect them. In your words: 'Where there is
genuine encounter between men, where one becomes another's friend, where a genuine conversation develops that
broadens the soul—there elemental joy and elemental grati-
tude well up spontaneously in the heart, and there we feel that
in some way "God" takes part.' I myself am inclined to express what you have in mind in even more concrete ways,
right down into everyday practicalities. For instance, when
family lunch passes harmoniously and in peace, when Sunday
breakfast can be eaten in a peaceful holiday spirit, when I
succeed in being 'human' with my next-door neighbors (who
are often so totally strange to me); when friends and acquaint-
ances have been invited and a conversation develops that hits
the mark; when a few people get together, and conviviality or
dancing gives rise to an atmosphere that binds them all together and makes them glad . . . those are the points where we
can in anticipation perceive the *eschaton*, taste 'heaven,' and
experience God. This may sound shocking to many people,
they may think us mad, because these are tones as new and
unfamiliar as electronic music. But more and more people
have the same experience. There are healing forces in such
community whose effects linger: after a successful evening
with friends it is easier to be kind to others, easier to find that
basic good-will that is necessary if one is to let one's house-
mates, children, colleagues, and neighbors live their own lives
without meddling. An inner drive is awakened which lends
wings to the day's work, or at least makes it bearable. All of a

sudden, the Divine work of salvation is brought out—down from the inaccessible heights of heaven, or from the unfathomable seclusion of the immortal soul, or from behind the barriers of the realm of the sacred—and is transplanted into the reality of experience, wholly tangible and wholly concrete. This is the visible fruit of which the New Testament speaks in connection with the Spirit of God. Of a sudden, all things are human. If someone is good to me, he does something to me that makes me good. If I can overcome myself for another's sake, I awaken healing forces in him. . . . In this way, all things interact and blend. The Lord, through us and through wholly human means, works Salvation for the world."

The spirituality of life in the world thus holds no basic problems for those who understand the life of the spirit in the same fundamental sense as the New Testament: as life in the Spirit of God.

What Albert-Marie Besnard considers new and wonderful in Christianity is precisely this, that the believer, in the fullness of his humanity, invades the fullness of God. "In order for him to approach God and offer spiritual veneration, he needs in no way first to forget his earthly existence and destiny, much less deny them; God's life itself is the substance of man's spiritual sacrifice; man's actions, his love and his suffering, provide the ground for that dialogue with God, for that never-ending and dramatic encounter with God, in which man's destiny achieves its peak." According to Besnard, the language in which God speaks to man, and man to God, does not initially consist of words, but of common daily events, and of those decisions with which the events must constantly be met. It is quite clear that Besnard speaks of life in the world from a perspective and in terms of a mentality which are

radically different from what often prevailed in the past. If I
read the situation rightly, the theology of the kingdom of God
is still the issue over which the minds within the Church are
divided. If that kingship of God, which is central in Christ's
message, stands also at the center of theology, important consequences must result for the doctrine of redemption; and if
it is central furthermore for Christian existence, then spirituality must be essentially worldly: then spirituality cannot
take place in a separate religious preserve, but must take place
in the midst of the world, where the kingdom of God becomes
actual as a kingdom of righteousness and peace, salvation and
love.

By worldly spirituality we mean more than merely that the
devout man must prove himself in the world as well; no Christian ever doubted that. Worldly spirituality starts with the
assumption that everyday life itself is already "divine service,"
and that the "world" is the scene and site, the *locus*, of the
encounter with God.

"The real converse of man with God," says Martin Buber,
"has the world not only for its site and scene, but for its
substance as well. God speaks to man through the things and
beings that he sends into man's life; man answers by the ways
in which he deals with these same things and beings."[6] I try
to express this by saying: things have a depth dimension which
only faith can see—their being is from God and toward God.
God is both the origin and the goal of everything that is. In
this way, all things and beings touch the Divine with the
fringes of their being, and the man who meets them reverently,
that is, who does justice to their reality, thereby honors their
mystery that is grounded in God (even though he may not
reflectively *think* of God). This world is God's world; God

himself is the ground that sustains it, and the purpose that gives it meaning. Throughout the world there is no nook or cranny where we could deal only with the world and not also with God. And the real point here is not to see the things of the world as parables and symbols of the Divine—we are not giving things a "religious meaning" of which they are in need in order to raise man's heart to the things divine.

That art of endowing things with a religious meaning was something in which the devout of the Middle Ages showed great inventiveness. They could not look at a rose, for example, without seeing in it the symbol of the Trinity: the root—symbol of God the Father; the flower—symbol of the Son; and the aroma issuing from the whole—the symbol of the Holy Spirit. No, today the point is that *everything* that is, is from God and toward God, and that man praises God (even if he does not know or call him by name) when he praises and loves the beauty of anything in the world—that he serves God when he deals rightly, properly, with the things of this world.

I want to stress once more that we are here dealing with a nexus of realities that is independent of consciousness or of reflective knowledge. Wherever and in whatever way man has to do with the world, he ultimately has to do with God, with him who is the ground and purpose of all beings. It is thus fully legitimate to speak of a "piety of being" when a man meets all things and beings in the basic attitude of reverence and wonder, even if he cannot see them as being from God and toward God. Such a man reveres God without knowing it: the service of God takes many forms. A man is serving God when he works for the brotherhood and solidarity of all mankind, when he fights prejudice and discrimination against certain groups, or when he gives his efforts to fighting hunger and disease in the world; and there is something of reverence for God in it when a man has an eye for the particular nature of the things and beings he encounters, when, for instance, he takes delight in their particular beauty and deals with them not carelessly and brutally, but with reverence and tender care.

But *Christian* spirituality in its relation to the world is not satisfied with such a piety of being, such an anonymous service of God. The workaday spiritual life, after all, means nothing else than to live one's entire worldly life in the Holy Spirit, which is the Spirit of Christ—and to do so in all areas: in one's profession no less than in society, in the realm of culture no less than the realm of politics.

Does this mean that there is even a "spirituality of politics"?

If that question surprises you, I believe you still have understood nothing of the theology of the kingdom of God. Is there such a thing as a Christian politics? No—but there is politics made by Christians. And it could well be that, in a legitimate spirituality of politics, certain problems of cultural and educational policy would not emerge as the central or even the sole problems. But does not politics involve fighting? Of course. Political ends cannot be achieved by religious means. Nor may a Christian remain passive in the face of, say, an injustice done to human beings. But there is one thing a Christian cannot escape even in the fiercest fights: when he opposes the evildoer, he must still look on him as a *human being*.

What *Christian* action ought to be like in the fight against injustice in the world has been shown by Martin Luther King and those around him, when he sketched and worked out the model of non-violent revolution. How far are we dealing here with a "Christian" concept—or more precisely, with the

concept of a political fight that Christians have decided to
undertake? The "Christian character" (I should not hesitate
to call it that) of the fighting program shows itself in the attitude towards the opponent. The aim of the program is not
to defeat its opponents but to win them to its cause. Christian
action of this kind means in the first place the self-purification
of the revolutionary. In the first place the revolutionary must
love. This love will imply firmness in going where the revolu-
tionaries are refused admission; it will imply accepting the
suffering, even the bloodshed, which will be inevitable, but
never *inflicting* suffering on the opponent. And in the end, if
the revolutionary goal is reached, there will be no defeated
side, but only the reconciliation of both sides.[7]

I do not know if ever a *revolution* was planned in such a
perfectly Christian spirit. What matters is that Christians are
ready for political battle, even revolution, without betraying
the Spirit of Christ as it is expressed in the Sermon on the
Mount.[8]

This is just one example of Christian spirituality in politics.
But it should make clear what we mean when we speak of a
change in Christian spirituality, from a primarily religious
spirituality to one that is oriented to the world. All of us will
feel that there is more involved here than prayers, pilgrimages,
and prayer service for world peace, more than "paternalistic
philanthropy."[9]

Open-eyed meditation

Today's changes do not affect just specific forms of the spiritual life; the change concerns rather our fundamental understanding of the spiritual life. We may indeed speak of a change in the very structure of Christian spirituality, which expresses itself primarily in the fact that today the spiritual life is no longer identified with the religious life. This does not mean that spirituality has simply lost its religious dimension. But once the place of the religious life within the whole of the spiritual life is given a new value, the structural change of spirituality is bound to affect the religious life as well.

Do Christians pray less today than they used to? I am not thinking here of those who are Christians merely by virtue of their baptismal certificate, but of the people who are convinced, committed Christians. If we go only by the frequency of retreats and pious exercises, and by the time spent in prayer —rosary, liturgy, and so on—we must admit that earlier generations prayed more, at least quantitatively. Karl Rahner, in an essay on "Piety Today and Tomorrow,"[10] has developed several "perspectives of a Christian piety of tomorrow." Christians today, says Rahner, live in an age that no longer allows them the luxury of a complicated piety. The true task of religious existence now, he goes on, is to live with the incomprehensible and silent God; to find the ever-renewed courage to address him, to speak into his darkness in faith and confidence and peace, even though we seem to receive no answer except the hollow echo of our own voice. If the Christian can cope with this situation, Rahner feels that Christian piety may in the present climate be forgiven for expressing itself less frequently in recollections and other forms of pious exercises typical of the past.[11]

We ought to ask ourselves, however, whether God has really become so distant and silent in our age as many people seem pessimistically to suppose. The reality of the world that can be immediately experienced, its tasks and needs which we must actively deal with and master, its ever growing beauty and splendor, are considered by Rahner an apparent hindrance to the immediacy of our access to God. Again and again, he says, we must clear that path which leads from our existence to the incomprehensibility of God, even though it seems to become blocked up again and again by the realities of the world of immediate experience.

Pierre Teilhard de Chardin seems to have had exactly the opposite experience. The more intensely he came to know and experience the reality of the world, the "closer" God was to him. His faith not only believed, it saw the entire earth, indeed the universe, to be one "divine milieu."

I am convinced that Teilhard's thought and writing stems from that "religious experience" which Rahner considers so decisive. There is no doubt that he was a mystic in the true sense—a man, that is, who had immediate experience of the

Divine. Rahner is right in saying that the courage to an immediate relation with the ineffable God takes more than merely a rational attitude toward the theoretical question of God, more than the mere passive acceptance of Christian doctrine. Tomorrow "the devout man will be a 'mystic,' a man who has 'experienced' something, or there will be no devout men." Why? Because the situation of tomorrow is totally different from the situation of yesterday. In the past, any personal experience and decision always found its way prepared by the convictions of the public and by general religious customs taken for granted, in which piety could find support. This supporting element is more and more fading away. The personal religious experience of the individual, therefore, is going to be increasingly decisive; compared with this, in Rahner's view, religious education as it has been so far cannot be more than a conditioning (of secondary importance) for the institutional aspects of religion.

How can man attain an immediate experience of the Divine? An old, tried and true method would seem to be spiritual *meditation*. That will not change. But the how and what of meditation may undergo a change. In the past, the *subjects* of meditation were, so to speak, the divine mysteries as such: God and his love of man, the life within the Trinity, the mysteries of the life and passion of Christ, and so on. There was an understandable conviction that we would succeed in contemplating such "subjects" in proportion as we prevented the world from disturbing our contemplation. Accordingly, contemplation presupposed solitude, withdrawal, and silence. The world had to be quiet so that the Divine might begin to speak. "Immersion" presupposes that all sense impressions are cut off as much as possible. The symbol of this form of

contemplation is the man who during prayer puts his hands
before his face. I want to call this form of contemplation
"meditation with closed eyes." There can be no doubt that
man may attain genuine religious experiences by it, although
the world remains, so to speak, outside. We can well understand that the "world," which today presses in on man with
an ever greater immediacy in its "growing beauty and splendor," may then be felt to be a hindrance to man's immediate
relationship with God.

But there is also another manner of contemplation—the
"open-eyed meditation." It finds God, not by turning its back
on the world for the duration of the prayer, but by turning
toward the things of the world in love and reverence.

What is in question here is not some romantic enthusiasm
for nature, but seeing things as they really are, not looking
only at their surface but immersing ourselves in them. The
insights of the natural sciences can only enrich contemplation
of that kind. It is assumed, of course, that our eyes look more
deeply than does the scientist's purely instrumental, causal
thinking. A man whose spirit is so modest in its demands that
its desire for knowledge is satisfied as soon as he understands
how a radio functions, or has grasped the physico-chemical
processes that govern photosynthesis, such a man will of
course not find "God" in the world—he will not find him because the true eyes of his spirit are blind. "The perception of
the divine omnipresence," says Teilhard, "is essentially a seeing, a taste, that is to say a sort of intuition bearing upon certain superior qualities in things. It cannot, therefore, be attained directly by any process of reasoning, nor by any human
artifice."[12] We need to be receptive to the enchantment, the
texture, the ultimate oneness of Being. Even if we should

finally succeed in explaining life in terms of physics, even then we would have understood only the physical dimensions of life. But life has also the dimensions of soul and spirit. And the man whose eyes have opened to that dimension may glimpse behind it still another, a divine, dimension: the mystery of Being.

According to Teilhard, the natural delight we take in life and all there is, is the first dawn of divine illumination. The appearance of the Divine in no way alters the visible order of things (so that, in principle, that order is in its physical dimension open to complete rational explanation). Appearance of the Divine may not be the right word: the great mystery of Christianity, Teilhard believes, is not that God *appears*, but that he *shines through* the universe. (Teilhard thus prefers to speak of *diaphany* rather than *epiphany*.) "Like those translucent materials which a light within them can illuminate as a whole, the world appears to the Christian mystic bathed in an inward light which intensifies its relief, its structure and its depth."[13]

Perhaps an example will make clearer what I have in mind when I speak of "open-eyed meditation." In 1939 Kurt Guggenheim published a book about the famous French entomologist Jean-Henri Fabre.[14] Fabre, it seems, was fascinated by the mystery of instinct. Instinct, which according to Guggenheim lies outside consciousness and is thus beyond the influence of the individual, represents the leading-strings that guide the insect. "Instinct is the opposite of intelligence; instinct is the intelligence of the Creator. . . . In the mysterious behavior of the insect which he observed, Fabre deciphered God's message.

"Fabre's research work was God's work, performed by

Fabre with untiring enthusiasm and unshakable patience. Re-
searcher and scholar, in the midst of his insects he lived in
the company of God. As his observations grew more precise,
more fully established, they became more and more a witness
to God." When Fabre, the author of that great ten-volume
work on insects which Darwin among others so much ad-
mired, was eighty-seven, someone asked him whether he, as a
scholar and scientist, could still believe in God. He replied:
"I don't believe in God—I see him."

If we are to learn to see in that way, we must practise open-
eyed meditation. To be, so to speak, submerged by the
"divine milieu" of the whole universe—that, according to
Teilhard de Chardin, is the fundamental gift for which man
can only pray. Lord, that I may see! "Lord, we know and feel
that You are everywhere around us; but it seems there is a
veil before our eyes. *Illumina vultum tuum super nos*—let
the light of Your countenance shine upon us in its univer-
sality."[15]

But does God need such prayers of petition? Perhaps it is
not God (who, as Christ told us, knows all our needs) but
the petitioner who needs prayers. When a man prays in the
way Teilhard describes, something within him changes. His
prayer shows how he has begun his search, and the more intensely he prays, the more intensely he becomes a searcher.

Nobody truly prays that he may learn to see God in all
things unless he is looking for him everywhere with growing
intensity. "Ask, and it will be given you; seek, and you will find;
knock, and it will be opened to you."

The change from a spirituality defined primarily in terms
of the religious life to one that is world-oriented is bound to
affect the manner in which prayer is regarded. Once God's

kingdom in the world becomes the center on which all things turn, man's responsibility for himself assumes a dominant position. In the past, the petitioner's attitude used to be more passive (God was to act and intercede with his omnipotence); today we see more clearly the radical unity of prayer and obedience, as Miskotte so well expressed it. Miskotte clearly shows that man in prayer may not assume the attitude of a mere spectator who only waits devoutly for what God may do. "Praying always involves changing our lives. Our entire existence is so deeply involved in this that there are times when we feel our complaints and petitions fading away in the face of this joyful and sincere resolve from now on to tackle some concrete matter in a different manner."[16]

Thus, says Miskotte, it is impossible that a man pray for peace and refuse to act as the conciliator in some concrete conflict; or pray for "our" daily bread without acknowledging that all men are brothers, who have a share in the goods that sustain life, and making an effort to promote social justice.

Just so, we cannot ardently pray that we may see without approaching things and beings in a "pure" way. The word "pure," I know, is burdened with many misunderstandings— the crudest among them being the identification of purity with sexual virginity. We here, however, are concerned with that purity of which the Beatitudes speak in the Sermon on the Mount: "Blessed are the pure in heart, for they shall see God."

Purity of heart

The divine milieu, says Teilhard de Chardin, is an atmosphere that is growing constantly more radiant, more charged with God. How does this "concentration" of the divine in human existence come about? In Teilhard's view, three "virtues" (his own term!) are especially important—and he mentions "purity" in the first place, before faith and fidelity. But this purity is more than mere freedom from sin, and not the same as chastity. Chastity, Teilhard declares, is just a notable special instance of purity. "Purity is the rectitude and the impulse introduced into our lives by the love of God sought in and above everything."[17]

"Pure," then, means something like "honest." We call a man honest who enters into any common enterprise, any task, friendship, love, or service with his whole heart—and without secret reservations or hidden selfish motives. A man who is no longer interested in any kind of knowledge that cannot be transformed into hard cash does not have an honest attitude toward the truth; he is not concerned with things as they really are, he does not want to gain a deeper understanding of their secret in reverence and love, but only to make capital of them, force them into his service. A man who looks on the human beings he encounters primarily in the light of what good or ill they may bring to himself, and what and how much he can get from them, is incapable of honest friendship or love; he does not even reach the point where he addresses himself to a "thou"; his regard remains so firmly fixed upon the "I" that he can estimate the other only in relation to his own ego. The dishonest man (the man who is wrapped up in his own selfishness) is thus incapable of any true encounter and true personal communion. He has no eyes for the "thou," the other man in his particular being. And the man who cannot recognize the things and beings whom he encounters, in their particular identity, is equally incapable of seeing the radiance of the Divine that they reflect. Woe to those who are of impure heart, for they shall not see God!

But it would be a gross misunderstanding of the changes taking place in Christian spirituality if we were to suppose that a more world-related spiritual life could be had "cheaply." Now and then, indeed, we hear the accusation that the "new-fashioned" interpretation means only that certain Christians want to shirk the strain of an intensive religious life. Let me say it straight out: to harbor such suspicions means not to have understood the strict demands of the Sermon on the Mount. World-related spirituality is concerned with God's kingdom in the world, and that, in all truth, cannot be had cheaply.

Membership in a "religious elite" does not necessarily mean membership in God's kingdom. Piety and fidelity to the law are not sufficient to establish the reign of God. Christ sets a seemingly impossible standard: he demands perfection in the measure of God's perfection. But what is meant is not at all a moral perfection which is necessarily unattainable for man in his weakness. Christ is concerned with the manner in which God is "good," is "kind"—he who lets his sun rise on the evil and on the good, and sends rain on the just and on the unjust. God gives freely what his poor creatures need, and does not ask whether they are worthy or unworthy. A man, privileged to know that he is held in God's gracious care, must also look graciously on his neighbor—and that means *this* neighbor, who needs him right here and now. "To love as God loves" means to love without asking: What do I get in return?

The demand of love is strict. I must learn that it does not matter whether I advance myself and my own interests, but whether my neighbor of the given moment finds room, a space where he can breathe and grow and be himself. Many ways of realizing love come to mind, but I would like to mention only this one: love realizing itself in listening. Does my neighbor (my neighbor here and now) find with me a "climate" in which he can talk himself *out?* The Christian of the "pure heart" (one who is not wrapped up in his selfishness) ought to have that capacity for dialogue whose development is so stunted in most people.

I do not mind admitting that it was a remark about listening by Rudolf Steiner which set me to thinking and became an occasion for an examination of conscience—something no Christian should ever try to avoid. We must accustom ourselves to listening in such a way, says Steiner, that there is complete silence within us. Normally, agreement or disagreement immediately springs up inside ourselves. It means that we have not completely surrendered to what the other person wants to say, but are occupied with our own pet thoughts. Everybody likes listening to his own opinion best! Thomas More made a mocking comment on it in his *Utopia;* nor, he adds sarcastically, ought we to be surprised: "Nature commands each one to consider the offspring of his own mind beautiful. Thus the raven caresses its brood, and the monkey its young." We welcome anything that confirms our own views, and respond with internal resistance to whatever seems to oppose them. A man who listens *that way*, then, does not have a pure heart. Wrapped up in his craving to find confirmation for his own ideas and notions, he remains inaccessible to the speaker's real concern; he forgets that even the most confused line of thought may contain something that is valid and important to the speaker, and that a genuine "existential" truth may be struggling here to find expression through these ideas and these words, inadequate as they are.

But, says Steiner, the man who practises listening uncritically, even when the most contrary opinions are expressed, even when the worst "errors" are presented to him, will eventually learn to fuse completely with another man's nature and to dissolve completely in it. And then, in listening to the words, he will sound the other's soul.[18]

No indeed, even in a world-directed spiritual life the Christian cannot do without the strictest self-discipline. Man cannot do without discipline generally, if he does not want to wreck his own life. The natural motives of discipline must not be underrated. To the believer, everything "natural" has also a spiritual aspect. This life on earth, good health, peace of soul, happiness, community, joy, and love: the man who knows by Whom all this is given, also knows to Whom he must account for everything he has.

There is no discipline without a readiness to practise renunciation. This is a fact that cannot change, even today. But renunciation, too, has changed value in the changed spirituality. Formerly, renunciation was considered valuable in itself; deprivation seemed something positive from the start, to wit, a sharing in the passion of Christ. The "imitation of Christ" meant primarily the imitation of his suffering.

Whenever things were going too well with a good Christian he became uneasy; indeed he came close to feeling guilty, as if the authenticity of his Christianity were in some way suspect. When life brought happiness and fulfillment he did not quite dare to enjoy it but tried secretly, by self-denial motivated by his misgivings, to salvage the sacrificial character of his life.

My remarks may overstate, but they do not misrepresent, the core of the problem. Yet "imitation of Christ" does not mean primarily "suffering like Christ," but rather "believing and obeying like Christ." We are right when we see in the Cross on Golgotha the tree of the world's destiny—but not because Christ died there so *painfully*, but because he died in faith and obedience. "Obedient unto death, unto death on the cross!" *This* is why God exalted him and made him "Lord," as Paul writes to the Philippians. Imitation of Christ means to follow Christ on his way of faith and love, even if the way leads to death. But it does not mean that the Christian does not become like Christ *unless* he suffers, that he becomes Christlike *only* by suffering. Christ did not seek out suffering. He was anything but an ascetic. So freely did he take part in festive meals that his enemies vilified him as a "glutton" and a "drunkard" (Mt. 11:19). "Renunciation" is by no means more perfect than "enjoyment." There is only one perfect thing in the world, and that is love. The better something serves love, the more perfect it is.

The suffering of man, and of the Christian, too, thus is always touched by a certain ambivalence. "If I give away all I have, and if I deliver my body to be burned, but have not love, I gain nothing" (1 Cor. 13:3). Heinrich Schlier comments: "This means that even the surrender of all property, and of one's life in voluntary martyrdom for Christ, does not render man 'profitable' in God's eyes—without love. Indeed, man does at times surrender himself in order to escape from love."[19] We should, therefore, be a little more tentative with our answers to the question about the meaning of suffering as such. Concerning the purpose of suffering in the world, it is best to preserve silence. But something can perhaps be said about the *function* of suffering in the life of man.

Although we do not understand the reasons, it is a fact of experience that without suffering man does not grow into a fully mature—that is, a truly loving—person. A life that is completely free of suffering—if there is such a thing—or too comfortable, weakens his vitality. Children and young people, for example, whose lives have been kept free of all difficulties, begin to seek adventure and danger on their own. A person who has never known sorrow, pain, and suffering turns into a childish, callow egoist. There is avoidable suffering, of course, such as stems from my own stupidity or from the thoughtlessness or malice of my fellows. And there is excessive suffering, which may break a man—not so much because it is too great, too unbearable, but because there is no compassionate and helpful brother by the sufferer's side. Even so it holds true that no man becomes completely the man he can and ought to be unless he has known and suffered sorrow, distress, fear,

and deprivation. Man happens to be so constructed that his
depths are opened, his human maturity and kindness and understanding achieved, only after he has gone through many
experiences of sorrow, suffering, even guilt. Despite all this,
human suffering is not valuable in itself. God's joy is more
powerful than any distress, life in him is superior to death in
any form. The hope which rules the Christian faith is that
Easter is God's answer to the Crucifixion. And Easter means:
Christ lives! From the resurrected Christ, currents of vital
force stream into those who entrust themselves to this living
Christ, as did the men who two thousand years ago trusted
in his love: Peter became a different person when he was
called to become Christ's successor, Zacchaeus came to his
senses when he was told, "I must stay at your house today!",
and the prostitute took new courage for a new life because
he had given her back her self-respect, had not recoiled but
had accepted her gestures of love. In these hearts something
had changed!

The vital force of the resurrected Christ, experienced in the
midst of the world, fills the world with unfathomed possibilities of happiness. How could it then be supposed that a man
could be most pleasing to God when he, out of sheer piety,
steps on the rose, in a manner of speaking, and pins the thorns
to his lapel! Joy, to be sure, presupposes discipline; there is no
happiness without the readiness to practise the necessary renunciation.

In fact, it is not possible for a man to have joy without self-
discipline. A gourmet cannot be a glutton. He must control
himself to savor his dishes. Most people lack the discipline
that is needed really to enjoy food—they greedily gulp down
whatever there is. And I do not believe it is saying too much

that the daily pleasures of the table are not the least among the joys of daily life. They are an entirely legitimate enjoyment; they are unmistakably part of man's natural equipment; then why should the Creator be "offended" if a man thinks them attractive, and worth the trouble taken in the kitchen?

If we are to taste life in all its richness, beauty, and depth of mystery, to the full, we must have discipline—the strength to practise the necessary discipline. A spoiled, hung-over Sunday morning is perhaps too high a price for a Saturday night which turned out a little too alcoholic. All right: now and then we gladly pay the price. But lack of discipline may become ingrained to a point where it rules every day, and in the end wrecks one's life! We need only think of high blood pressure from too much eating, or twitching nerves from too much smoking, or a mind troubled because of lack of sleep. Radio, television, newspapers and magazines, movies, shows can enrich life. But we may also impoverish ourselves spiritually and mentally if we live only passively, no longer in our own activities. The life of mind and soul dies when a man no longer knows himself, when he no longer has time for reflection. How can the spiritual life in the world thrive if we just live along on the surface, and take no thought of the "divine milieu" of all reality?

It could of course be objected that these arguments are far too "worldly" and smack of mere reasonableness. But in a world-directed spirituality, reason must play an essential part. The point is to do justice to the conditions of the world, of man, of life, and so to "obey" the Creator.

In "Piety Today and Tomorrow," Karl Rahner takes the view that the "new manner of Christian asceticism" is marked precisely by "reasonable behavior." Active asceticism, he says, used to have the character of an extraordinary addition to life, while today "it rather has the character of a responsible freedom in the face of obligation." This remark will disturb no one who has understood that the new Christian spirituality is above all concerned with the rightness of life, of man, of the world—concerned that God's will be done not only in "heaven" but also on "earth." "God's grace does not compete with man and his potentialities and understanding. For the Christian, the structure of the world, character, intelligence, and moral forces are not changed once and for all in a *divine way*. With the love poured into his heart, man must find his way in the world *in a human way*."[20]

Fully a man

World-directed spirituality—living our common daily lives in the spirit of Christ—claims all of our faculties to the full. The extraordinary and uncommon performance of the saints, which former generations found so fascinating, no longer impresses us today. Does this mean we are lacking in generosity and broadmindedness, are a little narrow and petty? Should we regret that our world-directed spirituality does not possess that "image of the extraordinary and heroic" which, as Karl Rahner says in "Piety Today and Tomorrow," characterized the ascetic ideal of past centuries? Let me say only this: if we look on the credit side as well as on the debit side, there can be no doubt that on balance the development is to the good. What matters, after all, is that Christians learn more and more to find God *in* the world, and recognize that, apart from a special call from God, everyday life, lived rightly, is the divine service intended for them from the first.

Thérèse of Lisieux, incidentally, had already rediscovered certain essential facets of the new spirituality and given them expression by her life. She remained in many respects a captive of the spiritual world from which she came; but her "little way," on the other hand, surely represented a spiritual and ascetic "revolution." She herself was very much aware of this fact, as is shown by the bold and unshakable firmness of her sense of mission. It is no accident that many people think of Thérèse as *the* saint of the twentieth century, and that she is the favorite saint not only of the so-called "common people" but of many intellectuals as well.

The new spirituality had many precursors, of course. The Hasidic movement may, indeed must, be mentioned in this connection; among the Jews of Eastern Europe, some two hundred years ago, certain impulses sprang up and became active which are altogether central to our "modern" spirituality. We Christians can only profit from the lessons which the Hasidim have to teach us about what worldly piety is like.

Martin Buber, by his persistent labor through whole decades, indeed a lifetime, has tracked down the Hasidic tradition and made it available to us. "The word 'Hasid' means a pious man," Buber writes, "but what is meant here is a piety of the world. Hasidism is not pietism. . . . It takes the beyond into the here and now, and lets it act and shape the here and now, as the soul shapes the body."[21]

Accordingly, the meaning of life, the fulfillment of human existence, must always be sought in the place where each man is living here and now. "Here Where One Stands" is a chapter title in Buber's *The Way of Man according to the Teachings of Hasidism*.[22] He starts out with the story of Eisik, son of Jekel of Cracow, a story Rabbi Bunam liked to tell to young men calling on him for the first time. Eisik, after years of abject poverty, dreams many times in succession that he

should dig for treasure under the bridge in Prague which leads
to the Royal Palace. He sets out for Prague. When he arrives,
a captain asks him what he is looking for under the bridge.
Eisik tells him of his dream. The captain laughs. Eisik has
come to Prague just because of a dream? Then he, the captain,
ought to have gone to Cracow—because he, too, has had a
dream, to go to Cracow and ask for a man named Eisik, son
of Jekel, behind whose stove he would find buried treasure.
Eisik bows silently, hurries home, and digs up the treasure
behind his stove. "Take this story to heart," Rabbi Bunam
used to add, "and make what it says your own: There is something you cannot find anywhere in the world, not even at the
zaddik's, and there is, nevertheless, a place where you can
find it." And Buber adds: "The place in which the treasure
can be found is the place where you are standing."

Most people have the vague feeling that they are missing
something, that their lives are not truly fulfilled; they have the
idea that they can find meaning and fulfillment somewhere
else (in another job, another marriage, another town)—anywhere except where they are standing. But the treasure can be
found here, and, special vocation apart, nowhere else! The
world around me where I am, the situations that define my
fate, the very things that come to encounter me today and
make their claims on me—*there* is my task, there the fulfillment of life available to *me*. In other words: I can find him
who at each given moment makes a claim on me, who at each
given moment fulfills my life—God—"here where I stand."
There is a little legend which reads like a parallel to the
Hasidic tale of Eisik of Cracow: "There were once two monks
who read in an ancient book that there was a place at the end

of the world where heaven and earth touch. They decided to look for that place, and not to turn back until they had found it. They wandered all through the world, braved countless dangers, suffered every kind of hardship that a journey through the whole world brings with it, and every kind of temptation that can turn a man from his purpose. They had read that there was a door in that place where they would only have to knock and be with God. At last they found what they had been looking for; they knocked; they trembled as the door opened—and when they passed through it, they stood at home in their own cell. Then they understood that the place where heaven and earth touch is on this earth, on the spot God has assigned to us."

This place where we are standing is where we must encounter God. This perspective, so characteristic of the new spirituality, is supplemented by another: we are called to serve God just as we are. This, too, Hasidic piety had understood and practised long ago. "The true sanctification of a man is the sanctification of what is human in him," says Buber. "This is why the Biblical commandment 'You shall be holy men to me' (Lev. 20:26) was interpreted by the Hasidim thus: 'Humanly holy you shall be to me.' "[23] To be humanly holy means not only to be fully and truly human, but also to be fully and truly myself (to become myself). Therefore, a man becomes "holy"—and holy "to me," that is, in the face of God—when he is fully the man he is. A Maggid has said: "It is the duty of every person in Israel to know and consider that he is unique in the world in his particular character and that there has never been anyone like him in the world, for if there had been someone like him, there would have been no need for him to be in the world. Every single man is a new thing in the world, and is called to fulfill his particularity in this world."[24] Rabbi Zosya has expressed the same thing perhaps even more compellingly: "In the world to come, I shall not be asked: 'Why were you not Moses?' I shall be asked: 'Why were you not Zosya?' "[25] Man cannot come close to the Divine, Buber declares, by overreaching what is human; man comes close to the Divine only when he becomes fully *that* man which he was created to become.

This insight is by no means exclusively Hasidic-Jewish; in Christianity it is wholly at home. Centuries ago Francis de Sales expressed it with his lovely simplicity: "I want to praise my Creator with the face He gave me." The thought is not new; what is new is only the consistency with which full, un-curtailed human existence is accepted as the standard.

We can see it in a certain critical attitude toward the traditional veneration of the saints. The objection is not so much to the saints themselves as to the usual stereotype of sanctity to which legend and hagiography try to conform their heroes. It might be expressed in a paradox: many people still love their saints as much as ever—but only after they have been divested of their "halos."

According to Roman Catholic canon law, "canonization" is possible only if strict procedure can establish that the candidate possessed every virtue to an "heroic degree." But while the Church thus demands "perfect virtuousness" of its saints, many Christians today do not trust such perfection, and indeed do not look for it in their exemplars. This change in Christian consciousness stems from the discoveries of depth psychology. We have gained a keener insight into the whole of man, and the depth of the person. Man's self is not identical with his conscious mind; what a man really *is* cannot be learned from his conscious attitudes and behavior alone. Augustine, one of the greatest psychologists among the Western saints, was still capable of thanking God that he was not responsible for his dreams. A twentieth-century Christian, too, knows that nobody can hold him accountable for his dreams —but he knows further that what is dreaming there is not a separate something but he himself. Alien as the dream-ego may seem to the conscious ego, it still is not something alien to the self, but is the self expressing itself in a dream.

The discoveries of depth psychology no longer allow man simply to disavow his unconscious; a perfection based merely on repression or sublimation is therefore no longer acceptable. It seems likely that the saints themselves had a much clearer intimation of their dark side, their "shadow," than their obstinate admirers of later ages have, who simply put it down to uncommon humility when the saints speak of themselves as the greatest sinners. The experience that we have gained in psychotherapy shows that man cannot simply sublimate by force the things that are at work in the primitive layers of every human soul. "We know those sublimating saints," writes Erich Neumann, "whose life, 'blameless' in the sense of the old ethic, is without a living sexuality, and full of love of neighbor—as far as their conscious is concerned. But our sharpened vision cannot fail to see the hellish aureole which rings that sanctity. Around the radiant purity of that center and as its integral component, we discern the garland of perverted sexual fantasies which the 'devil' sends to tempt it, the ring of blood and fire which, in the monstrously spiteful persecution of all unbelievers with autodafé, torture chamber, pogroms and crusades gives the lie to the neighborly love of the conscious, and to 'sublimation.' "[26]

I would not agree with Neumann that this dark side of the character of some of the saints "gives the lie" to the neighborly love of their conscious. It is true, of course, that any repression or sublimation leads to a split personality, so that love lacks wholeness, totality, perfection. But it is no "small thing" that love has been *practised* and surrender been *started*.

Nevertheless, after this great divide in the study of man which the development of depth psychology represents, there is no turning back to that naive admiration of the saints so typical of the past. Then, men saw only the conscious attitude, and could rest satisfied with the "heroic degree" of the virtues ("virtue" concerns man's conscious); today, we see more clearly the whole of man with all its diverse layers, and see also what is incomplete, divided, contradictory, dark, and self-centered in the "saints." The famous temptations of St. Antony seem to us to reveal less about the devil and his demons, and more about the monk; the crusading sermons of Bernard of Clairvaux show us with fearful clarity how much ferocity lurks even in the pious, all their lives, though they may never become aware of it. No sublimation can solve the problem of the shadow; even mere repression remains problematical. There must be a *transformation* of the "negative elements" within the individual. However, Neumann does not in this context go more deeply into the question of transformation.

In his Letter to the Galatians, Paul ascribes the transformation to the power of the Holy Spirit and man's response to it.

It is significant that he does not here speak of the virtue for
which a Christian must strive—though he admonishes us
often enough to be virtuous—but of the *fruit* of the Spirit.
"The fruit of the Spirit is love, joy, peace, patience, kindness,
goodness, faithfulness, gentleness, self-control" (Gal. 5:22).
It is a characteristic of the fruit that it must *grow* and cannot
be *made*. Can we "make up our minds" to joy or peace or
gentleness? In this area, even the most vigorous intention can
accomplish nothing. Here, the Christian must have trust in
the *dynamis* of the Spirit, and, last but not least, the patience
to grow and mature.

Trust and patience involve man's acceptance of himself,
honestly and without reservation, just as he happens to be—
unfinished, imperfect—and also his acceptance of his shadow,
the dark side of his nature. We must not claim to be better
than we are, but we must *become* "better." There is a vast
difference. The man who gives up ("I can't help it—it's the
way I am!"), such a man has no trust. And the man who is
reluctant and afraid to see himself as he is, lacks faith—the
faith that God's Spirit has the power to transform the "flesh,"
that is, the "nature," of man.

To Léon Bloy we owe this striking formulation: "There is
only one sadness—not to be a saint." But even this sadness
can become a temptation—the temptation to lack trust and
patience. God is great enough for man to come to him just as
he is. Therefore, why should a Christian be hesitant and
afraid to see what his dreams, for instance, reveal of his unconscious urges? Is he by any chance *displeased* with the Creator who has allowed man, the "crown of creation," to evolve
from the animal in such a way that man, too, still carries animal traits within him? Man as he *is*, is not simply a person,

but is so constituted that he can more and more become a person. What matters is that man, by a slow and surely often painful process of maturing, becomes ever more "thou-centered"—capable of encounter, community, love. "My shady side is a component and exponent of the shady side of mankind generally," Erich Neumann says, "and if my shadow is asocial and greedy, cruel and malicious, poor and wretched, if it . . . comes up to me like an animal, conciliation with my shadow is a step toward conciliation with my dark brother generally; by accepting my shadow, and accepting myself in him, I also accept that entire part of mankind which, being my shadow, is 'my neighbor.' "[27]

When a man has the courage to see himself just as he is, "nothing human is alien" to him. He will see a brother even in the neighbor who has surrendered to the subterranean side of human nature—a *brother* who has foundered on the dark drives and urges which, we know, are at work in ourselves as well. (Thérèse of Lisieux was utterly convinced that she would have been capable of "every crime in the world," if God had not from the start cleared her path of every stone of temptation over which she might have stumbled.) "Love your neighbor as yourself"? The true meaning of this demand lies deeper. Martin Buber has pointed out that literally translated it says: "Love your neighbor as being like you." "You are to love him not 'like yourself'—you are to be lovingly devoted to him who is like you, who is as much in need of being loved, as much in need of loving as yourself."[28] Therefore: love your neighbor—he is like you. Love of neighbor is not an abstract love of humanity ("in charity to all mankind") but the love of him who is my neighbor here and now—because he is standing near me, has come to me, and needs me at this very

moment! He may be a "social misfit" who comes begging at
my door; or a criminal in jail whom I am sent to help; or
perhaps a man just out of jail coming to me for a job, and in
his eyes I see the forlorn hope that somebody may still give
him a chance. Scum of the earth? Love your neighbor—he is
like you!

The apostle Paul sees men's bondage to the shadow within
them as a community of fate embracing all mankind. This
hereditary human nature is what he calls "the flesh." But he
does not have in mind only the sensual, much less the sexual,
side of human nature. "Flesh" is the way man is from the
cradle, so to speak, not just in the physical-sensual, but also in
the psychical-spiritual dimension of his life. Enmity and envy,
too, are for Paul examples of "the works of the flesh." The
Adam of the Bible is for him the first representative of man in
the flesh. Man is by nature inescapably caught up in the
power of the impersonal, anti-personal prison of his self
("sin"). By nature? Paul does not put it that way, of course.
But since every man is "flesh" like "Adam," he is caught in
the darkness within him, and instinctively centered on nothing but his own ego. However: besides the "first man from the
earth" there is the "second man from heaven" (1 Cor. 15:47).
Christ is different: in him the "heavenly" way—God's way—
is at work. Not a natural "self-centeredness" but a divine
"thou-centeredness." As Dietrich Bonhoeffer expressed it:
"Christ is the man for others." God, whose essence is love—
could he show his image more clearly in man, could he reveal
himself more radiantly in man, than by love? The "son" bears
the "very stamp of his nature," he "reflects the glory of God"
(Heb. 1:2). "Just as we have borne the image of dust, we shall
also bear the image of the man of heaven" (1 Cor. 15:49).

What makes this assimilation of the "man of dust" to the "man of heaven" possible is the Holy Spirit—that same Spirit which is powerful in Christ and active in all those connected with him. The Spirit lets his fruit ripen in the believer so that he may become capable of surrender like Christ—loving like Christ, and thus a *likeness* of God and recognizable as God's child.

The new spirituality is not very fond of the word "self-sanctification." The dislike does not spring from any moral laxness, but from the conviction that no man can sanctify himself, and that sanctity cannot mean anything else than that God's Spirit, the holy and sanctifying Spirit, is powerful within him.

Dietrich Bonhoeffer, in 1944, writing from prison to a friend, recalled a conversation he had had with a young French pastor thirteen years earlier. The two had asked themselves what they really wanted to make of their lives, and the other had said that he wanted to become a saint. Bonhoeffer recalled that he had been much impressed, but still he had objected and said that he, for his part, wanted to learn to *believe*. For years he did not realize the profundity of this contrast, and had thought he could learn to believe by trying to lead a holy life. "Later I discovered . . . that it is only by living completely in this world that one learns to believe. One must abandon every attempt to make something of oneself, whether it be a saint, a converted sinner, a churchman (the priestly type, so called), a righteous man or an unrighteous one, a sick man or a healthy one. This is what I mean by worldliness—taking life in one's stride, with all its duties and problems, its successes and failures, its experiences and helplessness. It is in such a life that we throw ourselves utterly in the arms of God and participate in his sufferings in the world and watch with Christ in Gethsemane. That is faith, that is *metanoia*, and that is what makes a man, and a Christian."[29]

Notes

1. J. Sudbrack, "Vom Geheimnis christlicher Spiritualität," in *Geist und Leben*, 39 (1966), 27.
2. *Ibid.*
3. *Ibid.*, pp. 27–35.
4. Hans Urs von Balthasar, "The Gospel as Norm and Test of All Spirituality in the Church," in *Concilium*, 9 (1965), 17–18. (New York, The Paulist Press).
5. See also "Zur Theologie des Rätestandes," in Richter, *Das Wagnis der Nachfolge* (Paderborn, 1964), pp. 9–57.
6. Martin Buber, "Die Chassidische Botschaft," in *Werke*, Vol. III, p. 744.
7. Martin Luther King's Program, The Southern Christian Leadership Conference.
8. C. J. Snoek, "The Third World, Revolution and Christianity," in *Concilium*, 15 (1966), 31–48.
9. *Ibid.*, p. 44.
10. Cf. *Geist und Leben*, 39 (1966), 332ff.
11. *Ibid.*, p. 334.
12. P. Teilhard de Chardin, *The Divine Milieu*, p. 111. Copyright © 1960 by Wm. Collins Sons & Co., London, and Harper & Brothers, New York; reprinted with the permission of Harper & Row, Publishers, Inc. Originally published in French as *Le Milieu Divin*, copyright 1957 by Editions du Seuil, Paris.
13. *Ibid.*, p. 110.
14. Kurt Guggenheim, *Sandkorn für Sandkorn* (Zurich, 1959).
15. Teilhard de Chardin, *op. cit.*, p. 112
16. Kornelis Heiko Miskotte, *Weg des Gebetes* (Munich, 1964), p. 32.
17. Teilhard de Chardin, *op. cit.*, p. 112.
18. Rudolf Steiner, *The Way of Initiation*. Various editions.
19. Heinrich Schlier, *Die Zeit der Kirche* (Freiburg, 1956), p. 188.
20. C. A. J. van Ouwerkerk, "Gospel Morality and Human Compromise," in *Concilium*, 5 (1965), 15.
21. Buber, *Werke*, Vol. III, p. 15.
22. "The Way of Man According to the Teachings of the Hasidim," Book IV of Martin Buber, *Hasidism and Modern Man*, edited and translated

with an introduction by Maurice Friedman (New York, Harper Torch-books, 1966).

23. Buber, *Werke*, Vol. III, p. 940.
24. Buber, "The Way of Man According to the Teachings of the Hasidim."
25. Buber, *Werke*, Vol. III, p. 947.
26. Erich Neumann, *Tiefenpsychologie und neue Ethik* (Munich, 1964), p. 115.
27. *Ibid.*, p. 92.
28. Buber, *Nachlese* (Heidelberg, 1965), p. 244.
29. Dietrich Bonhoeffer, *Letters and Papers from Prison* (New York, Macmillan, 1962), pp. 168–169.

3 CELIBACY

by Michael Pfliegler

TRANSLATED BY CAROLE TANSLEY

Celibacy as a phenomenon of the history of religion

When the question is asked: What is the meaning of celibacy, and why does a man voluntarily choose to remain single for the whole of his life?, we must not overlook the fact that this is not just a contemporary problem. The whole history of mankind and its great cultures has been colored by this longing, this demand almost, to be free from the instinctive pattern of heterosexual behavior. This longing for freedom from sexual activity in life is mainly of religious origin, which complicates matters even more: for as such it has a duty to respect man's natural and instinctive way of life, in its moral form, and yet, at the same time, to deny it on a higher plane, desired for us by God. In this sense of the word (Lat. *coelebs*, alone, single), we mean a celibacy that is not just a man's "lot," but a binding commitment, entered into for religious reasons.

Celibacy and virginity too are not just ideals within the Christian faith, or within the Church, for that matter. They are both phenomena of the history and evolution of religion. We must first establish this point.

In many ancient civilizations the sex act was thought of as something that made a man "unclean," and therefore, although both necessary and indispensable, as something sinful.[1] Herodotus tells[2] that among the ancient Babylonians it was the custom for the man and his wife to take a bath and make an offering of incense after sleeping together. The ancient Arab races had a similar attitude: Mohammed embraced it as the first and most ancient will of the Creator. The Jewish people considered that, after sexual intercourse, a man and his wife were unclean until the following evening (Lev. 15:18). The people of ancient India saw conception and birth as being closely bound up with the certainty of death. The goddess of lasciviousness is Bhavari, but she is also the goddess of Death and Destruction. Among the islanders of Fiji and some of the Red Indian tribes, a man and woman are not permitted to live together under the same roof, even after marriage; only the occasional stolen meeting is allowed. The very fact that the sexual instinct was so strong and overpowering made many races regard it as inspired by devils; under the influence of this force a man was in the power of evil spirits.[3] "It was ancient Red Indian tribal law that any man who had scalped an enemy must abstain from eating meat or from touching a woman for six months; otherwise he would be killed by the spirit of the dead man."[4]

St. Paul commends intercourse within marriage (1 Cor. 7:5), so that Satan may not lead the man and his wife into temptation. This is understandable advice from a moral point of view, but the mode of expression is still reminiscent of original attitudes and beliefs.

It is dangerous to go into battle after defilement by the

sexual act.[5] The bride's veil is a defense against the influence of evil spirits.[6]

Conversely, woman was considered to be earthly—a creature full of the influence of devils, and for this reason she was often excluded from all forms of worship. It was thought that the powers within her might disturb the workings of God at the sacrifice.[7] "Mulier ad eam rem divinam (= sacrifice) ne adsit, neve videat, quomodo fiat" (No woman should be allowed to be present at holy rites, nor should she see how they are performed).[8] How many after-effects this concept of woman has had, and still continues to have, even to this day!

The first occasion of sexual intercourse was thought to be particularly dangerous for the man. It was therefore a common practice for the hymen to be split open by an old woman, or even ritually by a priest or a stranger.[9] For the priest was supposed to be armed with powers which protected him from the demons. This unpleasant, and at any rate painful, rite was, however, often replaced and the danger made up for by abstinence during the so-called "nights of Tobias" or also by making a sacrifice to placate the demon.[10]

It is therefore easy to see why, in the ancient religions, there is a religious obligation to remain single, to celibacy, based on the incompatibility of priesthood with the sex act. The asceticism of ancient India was particularly misogamic. But because, in a society where so many castes had to exist side by side, the ascetic caste threatened to die out, a compromise was reached: every Brahmin had a duty to his caste to produce one son; having done this he then withdrew into a life of solitude and penance.[11] Strabo records the same custom among the ancient Persians. In the non-Christian sphere asceticism is at its strongest in Central America and in *Buddhism*. The Buddhist Dhammika Sutra gives this advice: "The wise man should shun married life as he would a pit full of glowing coals." But in Buddhism only the highest-ranking priests (Bhikshu) and the yellow-capped Lamas of Tibet are actually required to live as celibates, in spite of the words of the Buddha: "A man who is bound to his wife, family and possessions is more truly a prisoner than the man who lies in chains in the jail: he is also in greater danger; for while the latter may by some good fortune be freed, the man who clings to wife and child stands in the tiger's jaws: there is no salvation for him."

Bearing this in mind, let us examine the complete range of classical antiquity.

Ancient Egypt. Nowhere else in the Christian era was the ascetic life of the hermit so widely embraced as in this land and in its neighboring deserts. Historians estimate that between ten and thirty thousand monks lived as hermits or in *lauras*. Antony alone had up to forty thousand disciples. Six thousand hermits lived in the Natron Mountains. The city of Oxyrynchos on the Nile numbered ten thousand monks and twenty thousand vowed virgins at one point—more than the rest of the inhabitants put together.

H. J. Bestmann[12] puts forward a pre-Christian reason for this phenomenon: "The [ancient] Egyptian priesthood is to some extent the main root from which all the bizarre forms of Egyptian asceticism and monasticism spring." The "Inclusi" of the various temples of Serapis at Memphis and Alexandria and forty-two other temples to Serapis were celibates. Another order of priests, the Therapeutae, were pledged to live on a vegetarian diet and to abstain from physical contact with women for at least the duration of their period of purification, lasting forty-two days.

The Chief Priestess in Thebes, called the "Queen of the God Amon," had to remain a virgin.[13]

In ancient *Syria*, side by side with the dissolute cult of the Atargis-Aphrodite (Istar), the virginal Astarte ("virgo coelestis") was worshipped as the *numen virginale*. Her priests were pledged to celibacy.[14] It was much the same in Babylon. Similarly, the priests of "Great Mother Rhea," so called after her headquarters on Mount Kybele, had to live as celibates.

Greece. In primitive Greek religion Zeus was the God of Light, and according to Herodotus not only the foremost but the *only* God. His center of worship was in Dodona. Here the priests and priestesses lived as celibates. Most of the philosophers, from Thales down to the Neo-Platonists, remained single all their lives.[15] Empedocles said that only the celibate man could preserve his inner genius.[16] Epictetus counselled men to follow the example of Diogenes, who embraced nothing but cold marble statues. Plutarch recorded that Thales lived celibate, and that other philosophers had also made a solemn vow to God to abstain from wine and women for one whole year.[17] Zeno is said to have had sexual intercourse with women once or twice in a year, in order not to be laughed at for being a misogynist.[18] Democritus rejected the sex act as a kind of apoplexy in which a man started out of his own body.[19] Hippocrates called it a kind of mild epilepsy.

The *Romans* had no celibate priesthood. Marriage was actually a religious as well as a civil duty. The highest priest, however, the Pontifex Maximus, the Flamen Dialis, Chief Priest of Jupiter, was only allowed to marry once, and his marriage could be annulled only by death.[20] But the Romans did regard celibacy for the female priesthood as being of the highest importance. The guardians of the sacred fire, the Vestal Virgins, were pledged to the strictest virginity. The terrible punishment for a fallen Vestal Virgin is well known; she was walled up alive on the Campus Sceleratus. Her seducer was empaled on a stake and flogged to death.

The Aztecs had a high opinion of celibacy.[21] They brought up their young people very strictly in a kind of seminary until they reached a marriageable age: then, on the feast of the God Tozkatlipoka, they were released. Anyone who was still not married at the age of twenty-two years was regarded as wanting to devote his life to the service of the temple. The temple priests lived in celibacy, with the most severe consequences: for if one of them later regretted having chosen a celibate life, he was scorned by everyone, and no woman was prepared to take him in marriage. There were a great many temple priests. According to the records of the ancient Mexican kingdom there were four million celibate priests, and five thousand in the temple at Mexico alone. We now find it quite incomprehensible that such horrible cruelty could go hand in hand with the highest moral requirements: for these priests "there was a most severe punishment for any contact with the female sex: to be whipped to death. Whenever they met a woman they had to lower their eyes to the ground. The Chief Priest was not even allowed to leave the temple, or to come into contact with woman in any way, not even socially. If he violated these laws, his body was torn to pieces and his limbs given to his successor as a warning example."[22]

There were also Vestal Virgins in ancient Mexico; it was their task to guard the sacred fire, just as in Rome. Many remained within the order throughout their lives, others for a few years only. There were religious orders of men and women where the vows were taken at the age of seven. Among the Incas of Peru there was the order of the Sunbrides; they were selected from the highest-ranking classes only. Like the Vestals in Rome they were treated with the utmost reverence. Violation of their vow of chastity was punished in the same way as in Rome—by being walled up alive. Only the "Inca," the Emperor (as the incarnation of the Sun God), was permitted to choose his queen from amongst the Sunbrides. Fifteen hundred of these nuns alone lived in the convent at Cuzko.

The Peoples of the Old Testament. After this summary of the great importance attributed to a life of celibacy and virginity among the people of other ancient civilizations, it seems almost sacrilege to have to say that the Jews acknowledged neither the celibate priesthood nor the cult of virginity as ideals; there is no trace, or at best only a very faint parallel, of the asceticism of the Brahmins or the *lauras* of Egyptian Incluses and Recluses, very little of the extreme respect shown by ancient Greek philosophers for freedom from the sexual impulse, no equivalents of Vestal Virgins, nothing which might be comparable with the Sunbrides of ancient Peru and Mexico. And yet the New Testament is built up upon the Old, inspired by it; and the same power of authority is attributed to the Old Testament (Rom. 1:2, 3:1 and foll.; 16:26).

What is there to be found in the Books of the Old Testament which could be compared with the cultures and customs of other races?

It *is* just possible to find a few recommendations of celibacy

(Prov. 31:3). For a man, woman is the worst danger (Sir. 7:16), her greatest gift is to remain an undefiled virgin (Sir. 9:9). According to the book of Exodus, sexual intercourse defiles a man (Ex. 19:15); the priest who offers the sacrifice must abstain from intercourse during his period of divine service (Lev. 15:17). When an attempt was made to find evidence of the New Testament approach to celibacy in the books of the Old Testament, these few and inconclusive examples were made full use of. As a result of this the true meaning of celibacy was obscured and twisted. Just as an example: "Whoever comes to receive the sacrament at Mass after being contaminated by the sex act dishonors and desecrates the divine service."[23] This state of affairs lasted right up to the reign of St. Pius X.

What can the Old Testament contribute to our subject? The rape of a virgin is an outrageous offense (Jdt. 9:2). Priests may marry only virgins (Lev. 21:7). The shame attached to rape could, however, be made up for by the payment of fifty pieces of silver (Deut. 22:28). Adultery was at one time punishable by death (Lev. 20:10ff.). But this applied only if the adulteress were an Israelite. Fornication with a female slave did not count (Lev. 29:20). On the other hand, polygamy is the accepted practice, even for the great figures in the Old Testament story: besides Sara, Abraham had not only Hagar but other wives too (Gen. 25:1ff.); for further examples: 1 Sam. 1:2; 25:43; 2 Sam. 3:2ff.; 5:13. Polygamy is so much taken for granted that even God is represented as referring to it: Nathan says to David, after his downfall: "Thus says the Lord, the God of Israel . . . I gave you your master's house, and your master's wives into your bosom . . . I will take your wives before your eyes, and give them to your neighbor, and he shall be with your wives in the sight of this sun" (2 Sam. 12:8–11; see also Deut. 21:14ff.).

Gideon, hero of Israel, was famed for his seventy sons; legitimate sons, that is—for he had many women and concubines besides (Judg. 8:30f.). Jephte had thirty sons and eighty daughters (Judg. 12:8). Abdon had forty sons and thirty grandsons who rode on asses (Judg. 12:14). But Solomon surpassed them all: "He had seven hundred wives, princesses, and three hundred concubines" (1 Kgs. 11:3), and the only thing that seems to trouble the writer is that all these women led Solomon into idolatrous ways: no mention of disapproval of this polygamy *per excessum*. Even taking into consideration the fact that many of these women were "presents" and tokens of friendship from neighboring princes it is still an incredible state of affairs. But there were certainly a few celibates among the great prophets: Elijah, Jeremiah. The Old Testament did not see the value of virginity.

It was not until the influence of Neo-Pythagorism and Neo-Platonism had infiltrated from pagan lands that chastity and celibacy became ideals in late Judaism. Hence the efforts of the *Essenes* to achieve pure community life. Josephus Flavius says of them: "They shun sensual delights and vices, they maintain a high standard of temperance and freedom from passions in their youth. They scorn marriage and take in the children of others, while they are still young and impressionable enough to be taught, and treat them as though they were their own. They do not reject the idea of marriage itself as a means of propagation, but they themselves shrink from the rank voluptuousness of woman. Those of them who were married held a three-year term of abstinence, and they have no more contact whatsoever with the woman once she has be-

come pregnant until the birth of the child, in order to prove
that they married for the sake of procreation alone, and not
for any sensual pleasure."[24]

With the weight and authority of the Old Testament behind it, the Talmud soon suppressed the influence of non-
Jewish ethics. The older laws had allowed a man four lawful
wedded wives (apart from concubines); the Talmud allowed
as many as any man could maintain. It was impressed upon
the people again and again that it was their duty to marry. So,
in summing up, we must establish the fact that, compared
with contemporary "pagan" religions, Judaism, or the Old
Testament, made the smallest contribution towards the introduction of the idea of celibacy and virginity. It remained
hostile to both these concepts.

Christian celibacy

What is meant by Christian celibacy in the Roman Catholic Church is the voluntary agreement reached with the subdiaconate to be bound by a pledge of celibacy. Accordingly, this can only be understood to mean an absolute chastity, even of thought and desire. This celibacy, therefore, coincides outwardly with the perfect chastity of the vow taken in religious orders. In the view of many theologians this vow is also taken implicitly on entering the subdiaconate. The distinction lies not in a different attitude, but in the interpretation. The purpose of celibacy is to attain complete freedom to devote oneself to the work of the kingdom of God. The meaning of the vow is virginity as a way of life.

The case made out for celibacy in the Scriptures rests on two main quotations. Our Lord gives the first of these in Mt. 19:12. The Pharisees have just asked how Gen. 2:24 should be interpreted. This passage reads: "Therefore a man leaves his father and his mother and cleaves to his wife, and they become one flesh." Now they demand an explanation from him: "Is it lawful to divorce one's wife for any cause?"

The Lord's answer to this is: "What therefore God has joined together, let no man put asunder" (v. 6). Moses had allowed divorce—almost, one might think, against the order decreed by God—only on grounds of "hardness of the heart." Then the listeners stopped short and said: "If such is the case of a man with his wife, it is not expedient to marry." And our Lord said: ". . . there are eunuchs who have made themselves eunuchs for the sake of the kingdom of heaven. He who is able to receive this, let him receive it" (Mt. 19:12).

What is meant by these words? Voluntary renunciation of marriage for the sake of the dawn of God's kingdom, in the service of God by the grace of God. There are those—John the Baptist, for example, and later on St. Paul—whom God frees from the need for marriage and calls to his service in a special way, himself supplying the power for them to carry out their vocation. Paul makes the words of our Lord clear to us in the seventh chapter of the First Epistle to the Corinthians: "The unmarried man is anxious about the affairs of the Lord, how to please the Lord; but the married man is anxious about worldly affairs, how to please his wife, and his interests are divided" (1 Cor. 7:32ff.). The meaning of celibacy is unhindered, undivided service to the kingdom of God. Its affiliation is to all, and not just to the small family circle (1 Cor. 9:22). On this point the Protestant commentator Adolf Schlatter adds that by the married man's anxiety about "worldly affairs, how to please his wife" St. Paul does not mean the kind of morose anxiety which comes from lack of faith, but simply the ordinary cares belonging to the married state which distract a man from the Lord's service. The single man knows only one object of his love, which claims all his attention: the Lord God, and this concern is enough to fill his lifetime.

But even Paul does not impose celibacy as a duty on *any-body*. The freedom contained in the words "He who is able to receive this, let him receive it" (Mt. 19:12), is echoed by St. Paul in these words: "I wish that all were as I myself am. But each has his own special gift from God, one of one kind and one of another" (1 Cor. 7:7). Marriage, according to St. Paul, is not a law for all men, but then neither is celibacy. Celibacy is a charism, is a gift of grace from God: it is not to be extorted from him, but is bestowed according to his own free choice. Whoever this gift of grace for celibacy is truly given to, however, for him it becomes anything but a misfortune, a senseless fate of remaining unfulfilled in this temporal existence—rather it becomes an existence full of meaning, full of real value in a total and undivided surrender to Christ, and thus to one's fellow human beings, in a freedom from many things that chain us to mortal life, and in a flexibility which makes us ready for any duty in the service of the gospel. This celibacy, freely chosen for the sake of God's command, is a positive protest against the ungodly secularization of man, a challenging and explicit proclamation that man has time for God. It is a visible, eschatological sign set up for the dawn of the end of time (1 Cor. 7:29, 31), the passing of this world and the ensuing creation of the new man, which had already begun with Christ.

Only in the light of the words of Jesus, and of his tireless servant Paul, can the true meaning of the priest's celibacy be rightly understood: as a voluntary, undivided surrender to God and his command in the service of mankind—as the work of the kingdom of God.

As a result of this freely made sacrifice and the elimination of such an important bodily function as the satisfaction of the instinct to reproduce undoubtedly is in man, through this sacrifice of the most natural love of all, that between man and woman, a feeling of emptiness takes hold of a man's nature at first. The whole dynamic, vital force behind this instinct and its satisfaction is freely and consciously focused on the work of God. This alone is the meaning and the salvation of freely chosen celibacy (Preface for Ordination). As soon as this concentration on the work of God's kingdom slackens, the emptiness rises up again and makes its presence felt.

This total switch of energy and concentration has parallels in other walks of life: there are scholars who are seduced by the eros of scientific research into forgetting earthly love. Philanthropists, great leaders of men, artists—they too have to make a choice and decide what is most important to them. This is no false *sublimation* of the sex drive, as Freud sought to interpret it, or Christian von Ehrenfels (a disciple of Meinong), who says: "On the other hand, it is a peculiarity of the sex drive that, when restricted by abnormal conditions, it often seems to work itself out by producing cultural offspring. It is well known that when physical satisfaction is denied it, sexual potentiality can often engender an otherwise unattainable increase in the capacity to experience religious and artistic ecstasy, feats of imagination and vision, even the intellectual activity of abstract thought and conjecture."[25] Something else is involved here—it is a question of concentration on a higher goal!

It is significant that in troubled times when great demands are made on the priest, and also when his position as priest is threatened, the strength and breadth of his task are best fulfilled and experienced. The more comfortable and idyllic a

man's experience of priesthood is, the more exposed to danger
it is from the point of view of celibacy.

Whoever tries to compensate for the sacrifice involved in
avowed celibacy by living the most comfortable or pleasurable
life possible has not understood the true meaning of celibacy
at all. Decadent times are characterized by this *inner* menace
to celibacy. It has its roots in the ease and carefreeness of life,
without anxiety or problems.

*Celibacy does not imply that marriage is inferior or in-
significant.* Marriage has its own particular function, its cares
and responsibilities. Celibacy is even less an expression of
scorn for marriage. Married people have their own value and
rank which has its root in the sacrament, and in the task
which God charges them to perform. They too may run
aground on their own distress and sorrow. The priest, who has
enough with his own burden, and derives strength from it,
should preserve himself from the cross of marriage (1 Cor.
1:27). Celibacy is daring to take the risk of directing one's
whole energy for life (*élan vital*, Bergson) into the service of
the work of God's kingdom, and it is only in danger from one
thing: the gradual falling-off of this original desire.

The danger which besets a man who has voluntarily taken
a vow of celibacy is not primarily an outward danger, as it is
often represented as being. It is not the secluded cloister, not
the habitual fear of the *occasio*, nor a self-imposed mortification—against all of which there is nothing to be said, so long
as they do not become the panacea for all ills; it is only the
freedom achieved with the true purpose of celibacy, the readiness for any task God's work may involve, or, to put it another
way: only a priestly life which is full and brimming over with
this work for the kingdom of God can make the celibate im-

mune to every temptation. There is an outward danger which the cloister and mortification try to remove. The *occasio* presents itself in innumerable guises, and a man must constantly be on his guard against it and ready to meet the challenge. But mere separation and seclusion are no protection for the secular priest—they are just not possible for him. Those who are sent out of the cloisters into the "world" are therefore in greater danger.

The inherent danger for a priest in being on his own in the world is that he will fail to fulfill the purpose of his priestly life—fail to attain to the detachment which is necessary to a "spiritual adviser." This lack of fulfillment brings with it an emptiness, the emptiness a discontent which can become intensified to the point of bitterness. No man can retain his balance if the life he leads is without meaning, spiritually empty. Dissipation as a way of life can only accentuate the loneliness. This inner feeling of being unfulfilled can be ameliorated by outward resistance that is really lived through, and not just mechanical; yes, even through failures. But then, his resistance exhausted, he may break down if he is relying on himself alone.

The priest needs a community, that of his fellow workers. Very few people are strong enough to hold out when they suddenly find themselves standing utterly alone. Loneliness is a danger. Satan singles out the solitary man and sets to work on him—he knows when his time is come: "All the advantages that Satan has over us when we are alone, especially if we are sad at heart, all the arrows of loneliness and desolation which no mortal man is capable of fending off, were put into the hands of the tempter here to use against our Redeemer."[26] We should   pray to this sorely tempted Master. Only with the help of this God-made-Man can we hope to endure. *The* temptation is that of "being unoccupied." Gregory once wrote, and with good reason, of the "sacrament of work."

The loneliness and emptiness need not necessarily end in catastrophe, but they can result in malformations of sterility: in the embittered man, the bad-tempered, morose man, the niggard, the eccentric in all his different manifestations, the antisocial man, the egocentric: and the by-product is often an antipathy towards any kind of co-operation in work.

Harmless, but even more sterile, are the types who are dependent on some kind of *substitute*: one tries to compensate for his calling by finding a hobby—which in itself can be a good source of occasional relaxation; he becomes a collector, a bee-keeper, a botanist, a horticultural expert, a good housekeeper, or he gains a reputation far and wide for being good company. Another buys himself a camera and develops a mania for photographing everything in sight. Someone once confessed to me that he was "a professional photographer and an amateur priest"; he was only joking, but there are those of whom it really is true. As I have already said, all this can serve as recreation and relaxation. But as soon as it becomes the basis and meaning of a priest's existence, the danger of disintegration begins.

"There is scarcely another sin which is so unpriestly, and which can blunt a priest's effectiveness so readily, as the purely external preservation of celibacy: it is like taking refuge from fulfilling the sacrifice involved in celibacy in a blinkered, narrow-minded life, or in an insipid and feeble aestheticism."[27] "This search for a substitute may often be quite unconscious, but it is perhaps the most actual and the greatest danger that celibacy holds for the priest."[28]

The only salvation is to return to the true meaning of celibacy: to concern and care for the kingdom of God—even if the parish allotted to the priest is just a tiny corner somewhere in the country. St. Jean-Marie Vianney was sent as a priest to a parish of 230 people. He found so much to do as priest and parson that at times he had only four hours left for sleep. Well, of course, he was a saint of singular greatness. But for every man the way of salvation remains: "Seek first the kingdom of God and his righteousness," the rest will follow of its own accord. The kingdom of God has, even in its very last representative, the parish priest, not just an extension: it has an added *inward* dimension. And this is something of its very own.

History and ecclesiastical legislation

The Early Church. It is not the "commandment" of celibacy but its claim and its spirit that are based on the words of our Lord (Mt. 19:12) and of his apostles (1 Cor. 7:28). In the early days of the Church there was no law, in the sense that there is today, although the words of our Lord and his apostles were as well known then as they are now. Some of the apostles were married—no reason for the Lord not to choose them. And indeed many of them remained married when they set off into the world to bring the good news of the gospel to all races and peoples. St. Paul asks the Corinthians: "Do we [i.e. himself and Barnabas] not have the right to be accompanied by a wife, as the other apostles and the brothers of the Lord and Cephas?" (1 Cor. 9:5).

This means that the Lord chose men to be his apostles, and did not take exception to the fact that they were married. The first pope was married, and his wife looked after him on his missionary journeys.

But it means even more that it must not be supposed that Peter misunderstood his master or did not obey his word. The compelling part, however, that charges us with a duty comes with our Lord's words: "There are eunuchs who have made themselves eunuchs for the sake of the kingdom of heaven" (Mt. 19:12), and this justifies celibacy. According to 1 Tim. 3:2 we may take it that the appointed bishops were married; the apostle wishes they were all married only once and were good fathers and heads of families.

The view that a second marriage is an expression of *incontinentia* is taken by many people to be an indication of the influence of Neo-Platonism. At any rate, in the first decade of Christianity—the time of its great heroes—there is no celibacy prescribed by law. When Gustav Bickell tried to trace and find proof of celibacy in the time of the apostles,[29] Fr. X. Funk came forward with counter arguments.[30] Bickell got his arguments from "Apostolic Church Ritual" (written c. 300 in Egypt) which he had published, and this referred to celibacy of bishops and priests as being "seemly, and fitting."

But the sixth of the eighty-five "Apostolic Canons" (= 47th chapter of "Apostolic Constitutions," written c. 380 in Syria) actually forbids bishops, priests and deacons, under pain of suspension, to leave their wives on the pretext of piety!

The synod which was evidently the first one to occupy itself with the question of celibacy is the Synod of *Elvira* (in Spain in the year 300 or 306). It forbade those in major orders to enter into marriage, or to continue with any existing marriage (can. 33). More research would be needed to assess how much this severity had to do with a sharp rise in the numbers of those entering the ministry of the Church, and this after the gradual falling-off after the year 300 of the persecutions of the Christians, and a serious slackening in the spirit of martyrdom. It forbade sexual intercourse to the clergy, but not marriage itself. Its decrees were somewhat puritanical altogether. They also turned against the admission of pictures and statues in the churches, against singing, and even more strongly against music at divine service. The actual wording of the canon quoted, 33, runs: "Bishops, priests and deacons, and all clergy in general who have altar service to perform, must refrain from intercourse with their wives, and are not allowed to beget children. If they oppose this, they forfeit their official position."

Canon 18 bears witness to the severity of this synod: "Bishops, priests and deacons who are found guilty of incontinence during their period of service are not even to be allowed to receive communion before death, because of the scandal of such a palpable offense." Let us quickly add here: the first ecumenical council of Nicea repudiated the harshness of this canon in canon 13; likewise canon 27 of Elvira: "The Bishop and the priest in general may have in his household only his sister, or his daughter (from an earlier marriage), and only then if they are virgins and are betrothed to God." Canon 3 of Nicea, however, permits as housekeeper a mother, sister, aunt or such others as could not possibly arouse any suspicion, in accordance with 1 Cor. 7:29: "let those who have wives live as though they had none."

The Synod of Elvira was only a private and individual affair of the Bishops of Granada and the surrounding districts. Its decrees were, however, acknowledged in the West, either explicitly or tacitly, as being authoritative. One provincial synod after the other accepted them. (This explains why they are to be found in the most ancient codes of law.) One of the first of these synods was that of Arles (314). In canon 14 it acknowledges the Synod of Elvira, though in the form of a recommendation ("Suademus fratribus . . ."). A synod of Rome (386) followed suit in much the same way. The Council of Ancyra (314) decrees that those in major orders may not enter into marriage after being ordained.

At the first general Council of Nicea (325) the West proposed a motion to declare the decrees of the Synod of Elvira binding for the whole Church. On the protest made by the revered blind ascetic, St. Paphnutius, bishop and confessor, the motion was defeated. The grounds?

1. The clergy should not be overburdened with too harsh a yoke.

2. Marriage was a sacred and undefiled state.

3. If the motion were made law, then those who were abandoned would be in great danger for their chastity.

4. The old tradition had required only that a priest who was married should not separate from his wife, and that anyone who was single at the time of receiving holy orders should not be allowed to marry.

The position of the Eastern Church remained as in canons 17 and 18. They are still standard authority even today: clergy in the Eastern Church in the minor orders are bound by the decrees of Lev. 21:7,13, and 14, i.e., clergy in minor orders may not marry a widow, a divorcee, a prostitute or an actress— they may only marry a virgin. The fight against the contemporary Manicheism in the Orient hindered all efforts to repress marriage in the priesthood. In practice, even the best of them did not conform to these requirements. The great saint and theologian Gregory Nazianzen (born 319) was the son of a bishop and took over the diocese of Nazianzus after his father's death. Only celibates could then, as now, become bishops, which consequently meant that in the Eastern Church they were appointed from the monasteries. If a married man were chosen and consecrated, he had to dispatch his wife to some distant convent.

A Russian synod in the year 1274 stipulated that only married men were to be ordained as secular priests. The *right* to marriage before ordination in the Eastern Church led, in many ways, to a kind of *obligation* to marry. When, in the First World War, all the seminaries of Lemberg were transferred to Vienna, the United Ruthenian alumni from Przemysl and Lemberg also came to Vienna and were lodged in Baker Street near the Jesuit church. They could all understand and follow the German lectures perfectly. A few weeks before their ordination, which took place in St. Stephen's Cathedral in Vienna, they went away and returned married men. I asked one, with whom I was friendly: "Did you all *have* to get married?", and he replied: "Not exactly, but if you don't marry you are generally thought to be aspiring to the episcopate."

The *Canones Hippoliti* (c. 500) are the decisive factor here: Any man who is unmarried shall not be ordained to the subdiaconate until he has produced a testimony as to his chastity from his neighbor. A celibate shall also be received only when he has reached the age of maturity, has been found to be an upright person, and has been recommended by a testimonial. The carrying out of all these requirements did not keep pace with the legislation. The Synod of Trullo (692) had to declare that the marriages of those in major orders were null and void. It decided that the continuation of a marriage, entered into before ordination, was forbidden only to bishops. The other major orders should exercise "discipline" (restraint) on the day of divine service (can. 6, 12, 48).

And what if the wife of the man married before ordination dies? General practice found a solution to the problem of this eventuality: If a priest wishes to marry again, he must relinquish his office and can be given some lower office in the church, or be placed in the chancellery. This custom in the Eastern Church is also adhered to in the Churches in union with Rome.

The Western Church. For the Western Church, in the year 445, *Leo I*, called the Great, extended the obligation of celibacy to the subdiaconate. Leo is also the originator of the dictum: "There is no need for them to leave their wives. They should consider themselves free from marriage, so that while marital love may remain, yet the business of the wedding feast may cease." Leo, therefore, recommended the "Joseph's marriage."

In order to raise the question of celibacy from the canonical to the moral plane, the demand was renewed that the *votum castitatis* should be taken before the subdiaconate, in the synods of Toledo (527), Orange (441), Arles (443), Adge (506). Deacons who were married had to give up living with their wives. In the Western Church the decrees of the Synod of Elvira continued to hold good despite the many reactions and backslidings which characterize the Church's history up to Gregory VII. The First Lateran Council (1123) declares every attempt at marriage by those in major orders to be null and void. Out of the 360 Denzinger does cite can. 3 of this council, which is reminiscent of the decision at Nicea to for-

bid priests to live in the same house with women who were
not related to them or who were not morally beyond reproach,
but it does not mention can. 7 of the Second Lateran Council
(1139), which finally settles the legislation on celibacy:
"Censemus, huiusmodi copulationem matrimonium non esse."

Canon law and ecclesiastical discipline had spoken. But this
did not remove the inherent difficulties of the situation. Means
of communication were slow and inefficient at that time, and
a certain tendency towards sabotage on the part of many people in positions of power and authority added to the confusion. Difficulties arose which the Fathers of the Council
could not possibly have foreseen: for example, most Germanic
races reverted from Arianism, and with them came their married clergy. The loneliness of priests in dioceses far removed
from one another, their helplessness in household matters,
made it impossible for these dictates to be carried out and
adhered to. In many respects this period was a *saeculum
obscurum*. Whether there was any truth in his charges or not,
the very fact that Emperor Otto I could reproach Pope John
II in the Synod of Rome (963) with turning the palace of St.
Peter's successors into a brothel is indicative of the situation
at that time.

The synods continued to hit out hard. The provincial council of Seville (592) declared sons of those in major orders to
be illegitimate, and decreed that they could never enter the
Church. Priests could, however, revert to the laity. If they did
this, any resulting children could become priests. The Synod
of Bourges (1031) decreed the same thing (see cc. 8 and 10).

The Synod of Pavia (1018) went even further as regards
the carrying out of these decrees and declared in shrill tones
which offend our sensibilities more today than they did then,

that children of priests were slaves of the church! The German pope, St. Leo IX, extended this dictate to include priests' wives (1049). One of the reasons for the assumption that Lombardy was the worst place of all in Italy in this respect may be that we have very few reports and records for Lower Italy. Because Guido, the archbishop of Milan who had come to the throne by simony, did nothing towards carrying out the decrees of the synods, some of the common people under the leadership of two priests, Landulf and Ariade, hounded the suspect women out of the priests' apartments. But the archbishop excommunicated the would-be purifiers of the temple! The zealous people were called *"pataria"* (rabble). The pope sided with them, however, and the simoniac archbishop had to do penance. The example set by the *pataria* was readily followed by many people in northern Italy. The decisive battle for the observance of celibacy began with the Synod of *Lateran* (1059), presided over by Pope Nicholas II, who was descended from Burgundian nobility, and who had previously been bishop of Lüttich and of Florence. He too called upon the people to help him in his task:

1. Taking part in Mass celebrated by a married priest is forbidden.

2. Married priests may not perform any ecclesiastical function.

3. Secular priests should also be required to lead a *vita communis*, following the example of the monks.

What happened after this decree was passed was the first real indication of the true situation: the bishops of Lombardy did not make these decrees publicly known: all the bishops, that is, except one, the bishop of Brescia, and he was practically beaten to death by his priests. Once again this led to a new uprising by the *pataria* against such clergy.

But all this was only the beginning of the purge. The decision which clinched matters was made under Gregory VII. His first Lenten Synod (1074) already makes this apparent:

1. The pope approves of the intentions of the Pataria.

2. The decrees of the Synod of Lateran 1059 remain in force.

3. The "concubine keepers" are suspended.

4. The people are called upon not to accept any rites performed by such priests.

The greatest reaction provoked by these decrees came from Germany this time. Only three German bishops came out in favor of these reforms: Gebhard of Salzburg, Altmann of Passau and Adalbert of Würzburg. Altmann was forced to flee from his clergy into the Bavarian Ostmark (the founding of Göttweig): the canons were thought of as secular priests with *vita communis*. In this solution he saw the reform that might save the situation.

The German clergy drew up a petition setting out their requests:

1. Had the pope not heard of the words of our Lord "qui potest capere capiat" (Mt. 19:12)?

2. The pope was compelling men by force to live like angels —he was trying to forbid them the way of nature. This could only lead to incontinence.

3. If they had to choose between the two, they would rather give up their duties as priests than give up marriage—and the pope could find some angels for his church service.

The gulf of contrast between the two points of view seemed

impossible to span. Even the supporters of the reform, Sige-
bert von Gembloux for example, later bishop of Vercelli,
warned against the dangers of appealing to the revolutionary
instincts of the people, and the danger of a schism which must
lead to extremism and rioting. He had heard of people seizing
Hosts that had been blessed by married priests, throwing them
on the ground and trampling them underfoot.

As Primate of Germany, Archbishop Siegfried of Mainz
published the decrees of the Lenten Synod, in accordance
with the law, at the Synod of Erfurt (1074). When he gave
his clergy a period of half a year in which to think things over
and decide one way or the other, he was very nearly murdered!
He was allowed to go free only after promising to petition the
pope to revoke the decrees.

But Gregory VII remained firm and unbending. The main
difficulty in Germany was the traditional lay investiture. The
majority of bishops were also princes at the same time, and as
such were invested by the emperor with the sacred insignia:
the ring and the bishop's staff. The ordination came after this.

In the Lenten Synod of 1075 the pope prohibited this
method of appointing bishops. Whoever continued with investiture in this way would be excommunicated; whoever had
himself invested by a layman would become *inhabilis* for any
position in the Church. Five of the German king's councillors
were also excommunicated for investiture by bribery, and were
summoned to Rome to make reparation. King Henry IV was
called to Rome to discuss the matter and offer an explanation.

The latter replied at a synod convened by him at Worms
(1076) by "deposing" Gregory VII as pope on the following
"grounds":

1. In his fanaticism he had succeeded in spreading the

flames of discord and dissent from Rome into all the churches of Italy, Germany, France and Spain.

2. He had robbed the bishops of their immediate and full powers given to them by God, and exposed them to the wrath of the common rabble.

3. He himself had sworn that he would not accept the office of pope, but had then taken it on, and was now tyrannically exercising its power over the bishops. (This much is true, for as Cardinal Hildebrand he had strongly resisted their choice of him, and had even wept—accepting it only when the people started up the incessant cry: "St. Peter chooses Hildebrand for pope!")

4. His association with a woman (the pious and faultless Mathilda of Tuscany is meant here) was a scandalous outrage for the whole Christian world. The apostolic decrees were being drawn up with the help of women (meaning, besides Mathilda, Beatrice and the empress-regent, Agnes).

5. Bishops who did not suit him he called sons of whores, and yet he appointed laity to be judges over the bishops.

At the Synod of Piacenza the bishops of northern Italy adopted the decrees of the Synod of Worms.

The pope gave his answer at the Lenten Synod of 1076:

1. The emperor is excommunicated, and so must forfeit his rank and title.

2. Archbishop Siegfried, the bishops William of Utrecht and Routbert of Bamberg, and all bishops at the Synod of Piacenza are excommunicated.

3. The remaining participants in the Synod of Worms are given a period of grace in which to present their excuses in Rome.

This was the turning point. At a diet in Tribur (October

1076) the German princes—for reasons which were not exactly religious—sided with the pope and declared Henry IV to be deposed. His journey to Canossa (January 1077) was intended to gain him a free hand against the princes through his release from excommunication.

After some considerable time the fight for celibacy was pushed into the background by the political upheavals in the Holy Roman Empire; the Crusades began under Urban II (1088–99). But the struggle had not been given up. The Synod of Melfi 1081 (southern Italy) gave the princes power (in canons 9, 12, 14) to make slaves of the clergy's women and wives. Their sons were declared bastards but allowed the right to enter a monastery or canonry. A new canon appeared which declared all those who attended Mass celebrated by a priest who kept concubines to be excommunicated. The unpleasant consequences of this, such as witch hunts for priest's women, were repugnant even to those who supported the reform.

The matter was brought to an end by the decree of the Second Lateran Council (1139), which declared the marriage of priests to be null and void. Only after this point in canon law can one really speak of priests keeping concubines. The old demand was again renewed: only those who had taken the vow of chastity should be ordained (Synod of Winchester). The Eastern Church kept to the decree of the Synod of Trullo (692): the marriage of those in major orders is invalid. The continuation of a marriage entered into previously is only forbidden to bishops. So much for canon law.

The papal legates in all countries pressed for the acceptance of and adherence to the central decrees. But a synod in Schleswig formally accepted all decisions of the general councils, and yet marriage for priests remained, and they continued to be married. Circumstances were stronger than the best of good intentions. In the north there was already what was called an "honorable" marriage for priests. The conflict between what was law and common practice was left for the "foreigners." Here we have a continual process of transition to the reformed rectory. In Lüttich the canons were still openly celebrating their marriages by 1220. Elsewhere, especially in north Germany, bishops gave dispensations from the marriage ban. When the dispensation was given in return for some small favor or token of appreciation, people called this the "whore tax." This shows what they thought of it. The Synod of Bremen (1266) took stern measures against this disregard of the law:

1. Bishops who give dispensations from the ban on marriage are excommunicated.

2. All those who give their daughter in marriage to priests are also excommunicated.

3. Children resulting from a priest's marriage may not inherit.

4. Priests who keep concubines forfeit the benefice.

Similar decrees were also passed by the synods of Valladolid (1322) and Valencia (1388). These denied concubines the right to a church burial. So did the synods of Cologne (1415) and Paris (1429). All these decrees miscarried because of the lack of good means of communication in those days, and even more because of the general attitude prevalent almost everywhere. As the rulers of countries had a hand in deciding who should be nominated to the episcopate, everything depended on their particular attitude towards the Church. But let us hope we may regard it as an exception that one Gregory of

Montelongo, a cynic appointed by the Emperor Frederick II
to be the Patriarch of Aquileia (1251–64), chose as the motto
for his episcopal coat of arms the words: "Si non caste tamen
caute."

Exceptions. In a few isolated countries, depending on local
and historical conditions, the papal court itself was more in-
dulgent: this was the case in medieval Hungary. The influence
of the neighboring Eastern Church was infectious, and marriage for priests was quite legal in this Church. The Synod of
Szaboles (end of the eleventh century) set down marriage for
priests as something naturally taken for granted. It decreed:

1. Priests and deacons who have married for the second
time, and whose wives were either widows or women whose
virginity had been violated, must separate from these women
and do penance.

2. Any priest who lives with a girl as though he were
married to her must deliver her up to be sold (as a slave).
The money from this transaction is to go to the bishopric.

3. Priests who are now living in lawful wedlock with their
first wife are granted a temporary indulgence for the sake of
peace, until we have had further consultations with the Holy
Father on the subject.

The Synod of *Gran* (1114) decreed in canons 31 to 33:

1. In consideration of human weakness we permit priests
who married before being ordained to keep their wives with
them.

2. Any man who was single at the time of becoming a priest
or deacon may not now marry.

3. The wives of bishops are not allowed to live in the
episcopal palace.

The Synod of *Ofen* (1278) followed the example of the Western decisions in its twelfth canon: living with a woman in quasi marriage is forbidden to all clergy, on pain of excommunication.

The Decline in the Late Middle Ages. No further attempt at tracing history will now be made. Only the reasons for the well-known decay that set in will be brought to mind and examined. The historical facts may be found in any textbook. The instability and general anarchy left in the wake of Avignon, its popes and the schism that followed, also had their effect on the question of celibacy. The succession of Renaissance popes that followed set the worst possible example, with a few barely noticeable exceptions. Small wonder, then, that the bishops appointed by them were no better. The pastoral clergy reverted to marrying openly and in public again; not just the secular priests, but those in orders also followed suit, with, as ever, a few exceptions. The report of an inspection inquiry in 1563 in Austria by the Enns makes the following statement: in the Sch. monastery the visiting inspector found nine monks, seven concubines besides two other women whom he notes down as "legal wives" (according to what canon law I do not know), and eight priests' children. One can only suppose that two of the monks had publicly married their "wives." In the dissolved seminary G. (whose heavenly Baroque church dates from that same period!): eighteen monks, twelve concubines and "wives," and nineteen children. In a canonry: seven canons, seven concubines, three "wives," and fourteen children.[31] If this was the way things stood even in the monasteries and houses of religious orders, if they too squandered the wealth they then had in this way, it is a fairly safe assumption that the priests, with very few exceptions, were also married.

It is, however, also obvious that the will to reform continued to survive, and the more conscientious of the clergy tried to realize the ideal that had so often been expressed. In view of the upheaval in the Church at the time of the Reformation, however, anxious efforts were being made to separate the essential from the nonessential. At the Assembly of Augsburg, 1530, the papal court of Rome had considered the position, and held out the prospect of marriage for priests, and the communion cup for the laity.[32] In 1532 Pope Clement VII was ready to allow the concession of marriage for priests (after the religious discussions of 1532 at Regensburg). In 1542 Nuntius Giovanni Morone went to Germany with this concession of marriage for priests and of the laity's communion cup.[33] But the revolution within the Church had already gone so far that nothing was gained by these compromises.

The Council of Trent, after many hopes of finding other solutions, produced a new way of looking at the problem, a new approach to celibate priesthood. In canon 9 of the twenty-fourth sitting, every attempt to waver from the path of celibacy was anathematized. This denunciation alone, however, would not have been enough. In this council the vocation, training and education of the priest, from the theological and ascetic point of view, were defined and laid down. This struck at the very roots of the trouble. The decision to found seminaries for boys and priests took a long time in coming in many dioceses—centuries in fact. In the meantime provisional measures had to suffice to help out with the problem. The priest's way of life as regards clothing, lodging and residence was revised. The various orders were likewise required to bear in mind the ideal of their seminary. Decrees followed concerning the conditions upon which a man might be chosen to be a bishop.

(It is just possible in individual cases that an ideal young man who feels himself called to be a priest may be deterred from realizing his ideal by the thought of celibacy, but in practice this is generally not the case. Even today in countries where the ratio of Catholics and Protestants is 1:2, the ratio of the Catholic, and therefore celibate, priests to the Protestant clergy is 2:1. In Sweden Protestant bishops have resorted to ordaining women in order to fill the gap created by the shortage of male clergy.)

Orthodoxy and celibacy are closely connected. The emperor demanded that the Council of Trent should first resolve the questions of reform and then deal with the theological problems afterwards. This wish was not complied with. Joseph Lortz says of this: "Real perception lies behind this interpretation which is, moreover, confirmed both in theory and practice by the forces most faithful to the Church. The theological confusion within the ranks of the Catholic Church and the doubts that had been greatly fostered by the Reformation were certainly the main danger. But the potential effect this theological confusion might have, the actual danger of its spreading like an infectious disease, is, to a great extent, due to the breaking up of the idea of priesthood, as shown in the unpriestly life of so many clergy. For example, the freeing of many who were then priests from the bonds of concubinage resulted in almost automatic acceptance of the correctness of their views."[34] Almost all of the leaders of the Reformation rejected compulsory celibacy (Wycliffe, Calvin, Luther, also the later German, Old Catholic and Czechoslovakian Churches).

Church law in operation today is to be found in the *Codex Iuris canonici*, and the fundamental principles of celibacy are in canon 132, 1–3. Canon 133, 1 to 4, deals with the question of women housekeepers for priests. It is self-explanatory, and there is no reason for abolishing it. May God reward all those who selflessly devote themselves to this fine vocation—often so selflessly that they are content to settle for very little, a situation which is intolerable under any circumstances. The "danger" in which a priest may find himself lies not in the aspersions others may cast upon him, which blacken the slanderer rather than his victim, but in the type of woman who is cook to the priest—as described for us by Henry Bordeaux in his novel *Le Fils de la Vierge:* "Perpétue had been at the presbytery of Saint Paul for years and years, and invariably passed from one master of the house to the next. For she brought up these servants of God and trained them in her own way of thinking, conceding some right to them only in the church." The problem today is that the priest has little or no choice when he looks around for a woman to look after him and his home.

The canons 2242, 2359, 2176 apply to a *contumax*. An attempt at civil marriage is punished with excommunication (can. 2388). If it can be proved that a priest was *compelled* to take holy orders, he may, after court proceedings (c. 214), be returned to the lay state. Every postulant for ordination must pray that he may fully realize the gravity of his step, and be ready to take it upon himself.[35]

Discussion of the problem

Scarcely anyone will now put forward the argument that celibacy leads to scorn or disparagement of marriage. And nobody in the heart of the Catholic people has ever taken this view.

Friedrich Wilhelm Foerster said to all those who doubted whether celibacy were possible or practicable: "Celibacy is the greatest safeguard of marriage. Why? Because all the sexual arguments that are put forward against celibacy can also be equally well applied to monogamy. If celibacy is a physiological impossibility, then so are many marriages where sexual relations have to be broken off for a fairly long period or perhaps altogether, out of consideration for the life or the health of the woman, or where a journey separates the married couple for a long period of time. If Protestantism does not energetically withdraw from such slavery to the natural instincts, then it will be lost beyond recall. Religion is being beyond and above nature in every sense."[36] The very tone of this exhortation evidences an absence of the usual recriminations between the two denominations with regard to this question. We are essentially in agreement with Foerster and respect what this Protestant has to say, as he tries to put himself in a Catholic's place. The Catholic world gladly received this defense from a non-Catholic and accepted Foerster's works as quasi-Catholic.

Today the Catholic position has become altogether more flexible. It has become possible, since the Second Vatican Council, to discuss and write about the question in a way which would have been considered improper, for a long time in the past; the issue has also become more pressing. Things are happening now which hitherto have seemed impossible. Married Protestant ministers, converted to the Catholic faith, have not been required to leave their wives or even cease to exercise their full conjugal rights. In the third session of the Second Vatican Council the epoch-making decree was passed that even fathers of families may from now on be eligible for ordination to the diaconate.

There is another factor which should be taken into consideration, especially today, for the very reason that it has not been sufficiently adverted to from the ecumenical standpoint. The freedom *from* marriage as freedom *for* the work of God is certainly not a belief peculiar to the Catholic faith alone.

Sören Kierkegaard, the great Protestant rebel, broke off his engagement to his beloved fiancée when he realized that the marriage could well hinder his mission: "My engagement to her"—Regina Olsen—"and the breaking up of our relationship is in fact my relationship with God—is, if I may put it this way, divine—it is my engagement to God." The great Russian religious philosopher and poet Vladimir Soloviev experienced in the ecstatic love he felt for his fiancée the infinite love of God for all his creatures, and in order not to be separated from *that* love he made a vow of lifelong celibacy.

Celibacy is today by no means a problem confined to Catholicism, any more than marriage for those who have been ordained is. Today we can see the decisions and decrees that were made in the past in a clearer light and can judge them more fairly than before. Today we know that the fight for celibacy in the Middle Ages, right up to the time of Alphonsus Liguori,[37] came from the notion that intercourse defiled a man, even marital intercourse. The investigations and researches of the Jesuit P. Browe give the best insight into the thoughts and feelings of these centuries. There can be no justification for celibacy from *that* quarter.

And yet those who, from their own experience, cannot seem to strike a balance between sex and moral delicacy are not silent either. Two witnesses are to be called, both non-Catholic. The first is Ernst von Düring, Dr. Med. Dr. Phil., Professor of Syphilology at the Imperial Turkish Faculty of Medicine in Constantinople from 1896 to 1902. In his *Sexualpädagogik*[38] Düring gives a clear presentation and elucidation of the basic physiological and psychological principles of sexual ethics. Sometimes, however, it almost seems as though he himself shrinks from his theory in view of his own experience as a doctor. This is what he has to say: "Everyone feels: demands are being made on us, realities shown to us, possibilities put forward for which we are no match, we cannot possibly meet such a challenge. Goals are set us which we will never quite be able to reach. We are told: sex, the sex instinct is in itself pure; but *for human beings the objectivity of an 'in itself' is just not possible*, every one of us feels that with man it is a question of something more than what in the animal world is natural, merely instinctual. The contrasts, the 'otherness' (!), the insoluble problems are very real for us, and rigidly defined." For man there is such a thing as "*sexual necessity*." What does this constitute for honest, genuine people? What does it mean for innocent youth? And for the necessary abstinence between man and wife? After rejecting psychoanalysis as a salvation he confesses: "The demand which has been so much pushed to the foreground today: take advantage of the favorable moment to indulge in the satisfaction of your natural instincts, with no risk involved, no consequences or responsibilities to be incurred; and the much-emphasized claim: man has a right to be able to satisfy this instinct, do not spring from experiencing sexual necessity, *they spring from the inner contradiction within man himself which he must bear, and the more delicately he is made, the more tormentedly he feels and suffers it*."[39]

If the doctor is right on this point—and, remember, he is a specialist on syphilis—then control of the sex life, and above all the desired or avowed freedom from it, could only be borne by a heroic effort, with many inner struggles and perhaps even lapses.

The thoughts of a woman, Maria Luise Enckendorf, are even clearer on the subject: "There is something questionable, self-contradictory, unclean about sex. It remains for us *the chapter* which can never quite be fully and clearly expressed, never quite clearly fitted into life. We speak too loudly and openly of it, and we whisper too softly. We cannot bring our social life into harmonious accord with our sexuality, we cannot bring ourselves into harmony with it . . ."[40] "Doubts as to the purity of sexuality are not just common to Christianity, or even to the civilized world, for that matter.[41]

Throughout the ages men the world over have spoken and thought of sexual intercourse as something vulgar and unclean —*besides* which they conceived of it as being sacral. The feeling that anything to do with sex is somewhat suspect is old and quite widespread. Again and again one senses that man does not trust himself where sex is concerned. The act of fertilization is connected in his mind with a feeling of being in danger—it is indecent, unmentionable, sinful . . . as if the sex act were bound up with degeneration and decline—decline from what? And into what lapses and mistakes? It is better, it is safer, to avoid sex altogether."[42]

Two non-Catholics have expressed their views on the problem: the doctor from the experiences of his profession which have depressed even him, and the woman from the immediacy of her own womanly feeling and experience. Over and against the reflections of these non-Catholics let us now hear a religious hymn to the physical union of man and wife, making them one body, which appeared recently in a priests' newspaper: "Joy lives in the spirit, delight in the body. Delight is spiritualized to joy in the knowledge that the becoming as one in body may assume symbolic character. Above all, the body of man and of woman bears witness to this. The male and female organs are made for each other as a key is made for a lock. Because all that is living should be unlocked, only living, and not mechanical, consummation is his rightful heritage, and worthy of man. In the open love of thou and thee man's body is restored to its symbolic potentiality and capacity. In the act of generation, I and You are experienced symbolically and find themselves made one in an overlapping We. The I is liberated by the You to We . . . If a spiritually inspired coming together and integration shines before your eyes in love as the peak of the common path you tread, then you will find the way of transition from the physical aspect of marital consummation and the ascent into the spiritual."[43]

What, then, is the truth of the matter? The passages which we have quoted, since they are expressions of such genuine experience and feeling, can be said to have a significance not bounded by the particular time of writing. We might discover that the truth of the matter is that it is subjective, depending on the person. But what is shown quite clearly is the difficulty of finding a healthy, hopeful approach to the problem, one without misgivings.

But a decision still has to be made. We have cited decrees made in the course of history which arise to some extent from dubious prejudices. The historical symptoms of decline could be interpreted as natural reactions, but also as misunderstandings. In both cases this would be conceding too much. There is always an element of limitation in all decrees, they are invariably colored by the times in which they are made; we may assume that the age, and the people it produced, did not pass them *mala fide*, either in word or in deed. The fact that his wife was for Augustine the last thing that hindered him in his radical decision to commit himself to God[44] is an example that on the one hand conversion and the resolve to live for God are possible *before* separating from a wife, and on the other hand that, after this decision has been made, the wife is felt to be a hindrance to the new life. To which we must certainly add in passing that it is an Augustine, and not some lonely mountain parish priest, who stands before this either-or choice.

Most thinking has, in addition to its personal side, the general convictions of its age behind it. It is usually very difficult to live in opposition to the spirit of the times, but even more difficult to decide against it. The danger of solitude —*vae soli!*—is a danger for the priest, especially in this world that is sceptical of religion, a worldly world. It can become a temptation to establish oneself in it, but it must be borne and experienced as a constant challenge.

There is the danger to the priest of becoming a caricature of himself. In the preface to a collection of the letters of St. Clement of Alexandria, Karl Rahner points out that the saint, who had before him the example of the hermits of the desert, well knew the perils of loneliness; knew too that celibacy can shrivel the life of the spirit. Without the knowledge of God and without the wisdom which comes from him, the celibate can turn into a misanthropist, abandoned by all love.[45] This can take all kinds of forms—hypochondria, covetousness, avarice, sometimes even alcoholism. These are all ways of compensating for the need of marriage, although the celibate would not acknowledge this even to himself.

The spirit of the times should not be allowed to dictate ethical norms. The spirit of every epoch issues a challenge to be contradicted, but even contradiction should not dictate. "In different periods of world history and various spheres of culture the selfsame standards of the ethical norm do not always evoke the same response and the same opposition."[46] The mass existence of today, and its almost planetary dictatorship produces mass thought which swamps individuality.[47] There is a timeless, objective, morally valid law. But every age fulfills it in its own context. Our judgments and decrees do not fall in an age in which tens of thousands of monks in the small oases to the east and west of the Nile valley lived on bread and water and a little of the green stuff that grew in the crevices among the rocks. Around our churches and in our parishes stand factories with many tens of thousands of workers and their clearly prescribed duties and privileges.

Ever since St. Pius X swept aside all the misgivings and doubts that had been hitherto expressed on *daily* holy communion for the laity, the justification of celibacy found in previous centuries must of necessity also diminish—as Heribert Doms (Münster) stressed: "After all the feelings of awe and reverence on this point have been completely turned inside out (compare the Second Lateran Council in the year 1139, cannon 2), and the blessed Pope Pius X has, with a bold stroke of the pen, authoritatively abandoned all these ritual demands of purity as far as communion for the laity is concerned, we shall also be doing the justification of the fitness of celibacy for priests good by setting aside the old argument that was based on the ritual demands of purity among the Old Testament priests—an argument which is, as we have seen, somewhat problematic and far from clear in its conception when the Bible is examined in a scientific light. Who will still be able to understand that for this reason it is fitting for the priest to forgo marriage all his life—a renunciation that weighs heavily upon him, while for the laity, who receive the same God in the Eucharist, this reason need no longer play any part?"[48]

Doms means to eliminate one argument by this, but not to "draw any unfavorable conclusion on the objective value and reasons for the existence of the institution itself."[49] In addition it must again be remembered that in the Old Testament the argument of cult impurity played a far less significant part than in contemporary heathen cultures, and that there is no question of a justifiable reason for celibacy from that standpoint. The Old Testament priests right up to the High Priest himself were all married. From what we have learned of the New Testament case for celibacy the question which immediately arises from the texts would need a thorough theological investigation to see whether, according to the teaching of Jesus and St. Paul, a *free charism* of the soul for the ministry can be made a *compulsory law.*

The argument for celibacy remains the life-long, all-day and every-day freedom and readiness for the work of God. "It has surely always and only been God's intention that we should learn to control our manhood in order to be able to serve him more manfully."[50] The priest's vocation runs in such an unequivocally straight line that Francis Jammes in his delightful novel *Der Pfarrherr von Ozeron* makes even the mother, who keeps house for her clerical son, realize that she is subordinate to him. This attitude means that the life of a priest is often set apart: it brings a loftiness and a solitude that is difficult, almost intolerable—in the face of which even the man soon to become a prelate in Henry Morton Robinson's *The Cardinal* finds it so difficult to hold his ground, that the old Cardinal is still beset by dreams of a family. The married priest is not just a figure of ridicule in Graham Greene's *The Power and the Glory* alone.

When the vocation of a priest is fully realized in all its multiplicity, it constantly demands the undivided response of the whole man. This continual occupation and filling of every available moment of life can be found in other professions, but as an exception rather than a rule. In the life of a priest it is the rule and salvation. The highly gifted country cartographer, Peter Anich, can do no other than forget Vroni Eglauer, the girl who was intended for him. Only his sister Leni understood him, and she shares with him his decision to forgo marriage so that he may devote himself entirely to his work. This is according to Rudolf Henz who, after a thorough historical study of the subject, portrays this Tirolean character in his novel.[51] Professor Weinhart says to his gray-haired "pupil" Peter: "You have chosen a different scale not only for your maps, but also for your own life. Now that scale is applied to you, and you must measure up to it and endure it if you do not want to make a mess of your own life. Ordinary standards of what makes for a happy life are no longer valid here."[52] No vocation reaches out for the stars as much as that of the priest. The life of a priest is only to be measured by *its own* scale; every man must, if things turn out that way, forget a Vroni, and should thank God if he finds a sister like Leni.

There is, however, on certain subcontinents a tacit understanding: celibacy cannot be observed here. This is true above all of South America. Willa Cather, in her novel *Death Comes for the Archbishop*, stresses this point: the rule is impossible to keep, for reasons of spiritual welfare. She describes a priest who does not observe the rule of celibacy, but who does penance every year on Good Friday in the most horrific way. There is for us something not only totally foreign but also horrifying in the thought and way of life of those who came after the original inhabitants of America. After travelling through South America the well-known Catholic journalist Erik von Kuehnelt-Leddihn suggested that the rule of celibacy should be relaxed in this continent; it was simply impossible to keep such a vow under the circumstances in which a priest had to work there in order to reach the people. The journal *Orientierung* published by the Jesuits, printed this article without any editorial comment, thereby backing this suggestion. Through such a relaxation of the law of celibacy, celibacy as a free charism would obviously not be called in question: rather it might even gain in authenticity.

In the decision which faces every man who is called to the priesthood by God, it is not a question of two ways of finding fulfillment in life, one of which lies deeper and therefore hinders the other: it is a question of the either-or of two *ideals* which are there to be chosen between—for only in one of the two can a man perfect himself.

The Prior and founder of the Protestant community of Taizé (a community of brothers of Lutheran and Calvinist origin) speaks out of his own inner experience in his book *Vivre l'aujourd'hui de Dieu:* "The chastity of celibacy is possible through Christ and gospel alone. If you do not see celibacy in this light, you are doomed from the very beginning to bitterness, to failure and perhaps even to neglect of the very work for which you are called. *Then the fullness of the Christian life, which is as great in celibacy as it is in marriage, is destroyed at the very heart of its being.*" The value of both Christian marriage and celibacy, he goes on to say, is in the fact that they represent a striving for obedience to the Lord of the Church and have as their object an increase in love. And if love of Christ does not possess our whole being, we cannot hope to experience the fullness either of Christian marriage or of celibacy.[53]

Here we reach the heart of the matter. All our thinking on celibacy, if it is not on these lines, misses the point; we shall be talking all around the subject without ever touching on its innermost essence. Before every man who is, now as always, called, our Lord and Master stands, as he once stood before

Simon Peter and, without one word about marriage or celibacy, asked "Simon, son of John, do you love me more than
these?" (Jn. 21:15). Every man who knows himself to be
called will, without fear and without calculation, say with
Simon Peter: "Yes, Lord; you know that I love you." ". . . nor
height, nor depth, nor anything else in all creation, will be
able to separate us from the love of God in Christ Jesus our
Lord" (Rom. 8:39).

Notes

1. J. Müller, *Das sexuelle Leben der Völker* (Paderborn, 1935), pp. 67ff.
2. Herodotus, 1, 8.
3. A. Wuttke, *Geschichte des Heidentums* (Breslau, 1852–53), 1, pp. 134ff.
4. J. Müller, *op. cit.*, p. 67.
5. G. van der Leeuw, *Phänomenologie der Religion* (Tübingen, 1933), p. 25.
6. *Ibid.*; see also 1 Cor. 11:4ff.
7. *Ibid.*
8. Cato, *De agricultura*, 83.
9. G. van der Leeuw, *op. cit.*, p. 212.
10. *Ibid.*, p. 213.
11. J. Müller, *op. cit.*, p. 71.
12. H. J. Bestmann, "Die sittlichen Stadien in ihrer geschichtlichen Ent-
    wicklung" (Nördlingen, 1880), 2; *Die Katholische Sitte der alten Kirche
    in ihrer geschichtlichen Entwicklung* (1885), p. 127.
13. Herodotus, 2, 46.
14. Herodotus, 1, 132.
15. J. Müller, *op. cit.*, pp. 156 and 139.
16. Hippolytus, *Philosophumena*.
17. Plutarch, *De cohibenda ira*, 16.
18. Diogenes Laertius, "Life and Beliefs of Famous Philosophers," trans. by
    O. Apelt, VIII, 9; VII, 13.
19. Pliny the Elder, *Naturalis historia*, 28, 6.
20. St. Jerome, *Adversus Jovinianum*, 1, 49; Tertullian, *De exhortatione ad
    castitatem*, 13.
21. J. Müller, *op. cit.*, pp. 74ff.

22. *Ibid.,* pp. 74ff.
23. Origen, *Hom. in Leviticum* (PG 12, 474).
24. J. Flavius, *Bell. iud.* 2, 8, 2.
25. Ch. von Ehrenfels, *Sexualethik* (Wiesbaden, 1907), p. 17.
26. J. G. Hamann, *Biblische Betrachtungen eines Christen* (Freiburg, 1939), pp. 63f.
27. H. Wirtz, *Ein Laie sucht den Priester* (Frankfurt a. Main, 1940), p. 29.
28. *Ibid.,* p. 28.
29. See *Zeitschrift f. kath. Theologie,* 2 (1878), 26–64.
30. *Tübinger Theologische Quartalschrift,* 61 (1879), 205–247.
31. For more information: Th. Wiedemann, *Geschichte der Reformation und Gegenreformation im Lande unter der Enns* (Prague 1875–82).
32. J. Lortz, *Die Reformation in Deutschland* (Freiburg im Breisgau, 1940), Vol. II, p. 272.
33. *Ibid.,* p. 229.
34. *Ibid.,* p. 216.
35. *Acta Apostolicae Sedis,* 1931, 127.
36. F. W. Foerster, *Sexualethik und Sexualpädagogik* (Munich, 1907), p. 53.
37. Alphonsus Liguori, *Theologia moralis,* 2. Vl. tr. III. cap. II. art. II.: "quae requiratur dispositio corporis." (The question here is that of disposition, of preparation for receiving the Eucharist.)
38. E. von During, *Sexualpädagogik* (Zurich-Leipzig, 1930), p. 216.
39. E. von Düring, *op. cit.,* pp. 126f.
40. M. L. Enckendorf, *Realität und Gesetzlichkeit im Geschlechtsleben* (Munich-Leipzig, 1920), p. 8.
41. See above, note 2.
42. Enckendorf, *op. cit.,* p. 9.
43. *Österreichisches Klerusblatt,* 97 (1964), 18.
44. Augustine, *Conf.* VIII, 2, 5.
45. K. Rahner, *Zeugen des Wortes,* Vol. 26: *Kirchenväter an Laien* (Freiburg, 1939).
46. S. Behn, *Ethos der Gegenwart* (Bonn, 1932).
47. G. le Bon, *Psychologie der Massen* (Leipzig, 1932), Vol. V, pp. 124f., 131.
48. *Osterreichisches Klerusblatt,* 91 (1958), 5, 35. Also H. Doms, *Vom Sinn des Zölibats* (1954).
49. Doms, *op. cit.*
50. Says the struggling priest Aucke in D. Ouwendijk, *Das geschändete Antiltz* (Warendorf, 1950), II, p. 216.
51. R. Henz, *Ein Bauer greift nach den Sternen* (Bonn, 1943).
52. *Ibid.*
53. *Living Today for God* (New York, Taplinger, 1964).